# SANTA'S VILLAGE

## GONE WILD!

**SANTA'S VILLAGE GONE WILD!**

GONE WILD!

TALES OF SUMMER FUN, HIJINX, & DEBAUCHERY
AS TOLD BY THE PEOPLE WHO WORKED THERE

# CHRISTOPHER DEARMAN

AXCREATIONS PUBLISHING

www.axcreations.com

AXCREATIONS PUBLISHING is an imprint of

Axcreations, Inc

www.axcreations.com

For information regarding special discounts for bulk purchases, please contact Axcreations Publishing Sales: axcreations@gmail.com

COVER ART BY JAMES HISLOPE

COVER DESIGN BY JOEY CAMPOS

INTERIOR DESIGN BY CASEY HOOPER

Library of Congress Control Number: 2010914920

*Printed in the United States of America*

First Edition

ISBN-13: 978-0-9844539-0-0

ISBN-10: 0-9844539-0-3

For Mom and Dad—

Hope my stories don't cause you
*too* much embarrassment…

# ✪ CONTENTS ✪

# ✪ AUTHOR'S NOTE ✪

The vast amount of memories that Santa's Village created during its forty-six seasons of operation could fill many editions of a book like this. While I sincerely hope that may be the case if this first edition is a success, I believe that what I've compiled here is a great start in showing the wide range of experiences and events of those lucky enough to have worked at Santa's summertime home.

Working at Santa's Village lent itself to numerous fond memories that are shared by myself and other former employees throughout the course of this book. Of these stories, many recall entertaining "firsts"—whether being someone's first job, getting a first kiss, a first time experimenting with an illicit substance, etc. Having the park serve as a unique backdrop to these new experiences is one of the reasons for collecting these stories. Another goal was to try to capture some of these fun and amusing anecdotes for prosperity, before they are forgotten forever. I know writing this book has helped me collect some of my own misplaced memories, and I'm grateful to be able to share them.

As with most chronicles of events, details in the book will in all likelihood vary depending on who's doing the talking. What you'll read are memories recounted from how each individual lived and remembers them. While some might tell the tales differently, everyone has their own perspective. Inevitably, time tends to wreak havoc on those recollections and perceptions of life events—especially my own.

In writing stories that involve myself, I've had to rely on the memories of days spent interacting with hundreds, if not thousands, of people over the span of two summers almost twenty years ago. I've spent many years living a colorful life since the days of my employment at Santa's Village, including five foggy ones in Carbondale during college (stories of which I'm compiling for my next book). Please forgive me if I don't paint absolutely complete pictures or comprehensive records of all the events of the past. I do hope I've at least succeeded in keeping them enjoyable.

Besides the quotes and stories submitted to me by others specifically for this book, what you'll read in the pages to come is what manifested from my brain when trying to recall entertaining details of my days at Santa's Village. While I tried my best to tell the truth—at least what is true to me—don't bust my balls too much if my truth differs from yours. I'll be more than happy to give you the opportunity to tell your side of things in future editions.

Many conversations were recreated, and some identities have been changed or omitted to protect the privacy of the innocent and those not so innocent (of which there were many). Sometimes I'll let you know when I did and sometimes I won't. But as they say, never let the facts get in the way of a good story. If any of these instances pertain to you and there are stories that you want the "glory" for, just let me know and I'll be sure to rectify it in future editions as well.

While I am not proud of all the things I confess to, and I definitely don't advocate much of the hijinx that went down while working there, I'm pretty sure Karma has already paid me back over the years for many of the adolescent transgressions that I was involved in. Speaking of which, please know that I in no way intend to hurt anyone by telling some of these tales. I went into this with a good heart, and tried not to spare myself any of the embarrassment—I hope that comes through. If not, please accept my apology now before reading. If that's not enough, also know that I plan to donate a percentage of every book sold to the Make-A-Wish Foundation as a way to help bring joy in the spirit of Santa's Village to children with life-threatening medical conditions. As a dreamer myself, I'm thankful to have the opportunity to help make the dreams of those in need come true.

It's funny how some things mean so much to one person and nothing to another. While some people I talked with could go on for hours about their Santa's Village experiences, others struggled to come up with any. This book is not journalism. It's about capturing a small portion of the millions of memories Santa's Village helped create. Good or bad, I know the two summers I spent working there went a long way in the development of the person I've become. The enjoyment I got from my time working at Santa's Village was probably the reason why I did a college internship at Disney World, and still try to live young at heart to this day.

So kick back, relax, and envision a hot summer day with the sweet smell of elephant ears covered in powdered sugar, along with a touch of the unmistakable stench of Voban covered puke, and let some of these memories bring you back to the days of your own youth. Hopefully, it will put a smile on your face as you read about the many ways that Santa's Village has...*Gone Wild!*

Christopher Dearman

June 2010

PS: Do me a favor. Go to your computer right now and compose a quick email that mentions the website address: WWW.SANTASVILLAGEGONEWILD.COM—and send it out to anyone and everyone in your address book that might enjoy reading about the fun, hijinx and debauchery that myself and others experienced. Not only will you be making the embarrassment I'm sure to endure by confessing some of these things worthwhile, you'll also feel better about yourself by helping kids in need as well.

BTW: I know the word hijinx might not be spelled "correctly," but I have found at least six different known variations - and I just think this way looks the coolest. Also, my lawyer said to print the quotes that were submitted by email "as is" – so besides correcting some blatant misspellings, I kept things pretty much how they came to me...

PPS: If you are a former employee and missed out on being included in this edition of *Santa's Village—Gone Wild!* don't despair. You can also use the above website to request a survey that will help jog your memory, and give you the chance to share your tales in future editions of the book.

# ✪ FOREWORD ✪
## BY PHILLIP L. WENZ

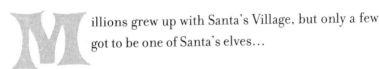illions grew up with Santa's Village, but only a few got to be one of Santa's elves...

Over 50 years have passed since the gates of Santa's Village first opened. As one of the nation's first chain of theme parks, the Dundee version, built by Californian Glenn Holland, was by far the most successful. In its history, the park employed more than 11,000 people and truly became a rite of summer for many local teenagers.

In many ways, Santa's Village was a little city within itself. Just as an incorporated community, the park was broken down into departments with certain responsibilities. Each department was headed up by a full-time manager who delegated the job tasks to the part-time summer help. The department managers were under the supervision of the director of operations, who answered to the park's general manager. And of course, the general manager worked in direct correlation with the owners of Santa's Village.

For many years, Santa's Village would host job days to offer opportunities to the local teenager to become part of the exciting entertainment and hospitality industry. This was quite an undertaking as upwards of 1,000 people would apply for the few hundred positions that might be available that particular year. Management would set up large interviewing areas in the Polar Dome Ice Arena to screen, interview, and hire the new "elves."

Once all the new hires were confirmed, a massive orientation program was conducted that included corporate policies, safety rules, and hospitality guidelines. After the orientation, the employees would be teamed up with a department manager to learn the ropes of their new summer job and to meet all the experienced workers from the previous seasons.

Once the park opened and the summer employees got used to their jobs, a sort of family community evolved within the gates of Santa's Village. The first priority for all was the guest and the tasks at hand, but friendships and fun were not far behind. The Management of Santa's Village encouraged team unity with annual events for the workers and incentives, knowing that a happy employee makes happy guests.

The full-time staff of Santa's Village understood most teenagers. A few of them started as part-time summer help and worked their way through college with the park. After graduation, they took on career positions. Other staff members were hired knowing that young people were going to make up their complete departments. Either way, the staff and management of the park knew the challenges of working with young people. They had to be supervisors, counselors, teachers, disciplinarians, coaches, and friends while keeping to the business of a theme park. Plus they were outnumbered.

On an average summer day, there could be 5,000 guests in the park. During a large company picnic day and a good gate day, the crowds could swell to over 15,000. The full-time staff, which never numbered more than thirty, spread themselves over the forty acres of the park to facilitate the operation along with managing the summertime help. As you can see, the level of knowledge and commitment to the park's success was rooted in the management.

During any given summer the park would employ some 300 young people. And, as in any other industry, company, or organization, when you get that many teenagers together, there is bound to be some hijinx and shenanigans. That's just part of the deal, and everyone who has ever held a part-time summer job knows it. So do the managers or owners of any company, as they were once young themselves.

Now granted, working at a theme park might provide some unique occasions and locations for mischief, but so does a large retail chain, a fast-food restaurant, and a park district. Kids will be kids and teenagers will be teenagers. That is just a fact, especially on one's first job. Pranks and stunts by 16, 17, and 18 year olds are not unique to Santa's Village; they are just part of the maturation process that most go through.

For most teenagers, the time they spent working at Santa's Village was the first time they were in an environment that was not controlled by parents or the school system. It was their first exposure to earning a paycheck and working with others. It was also the first time for experiencing some independence, discovering new emotions and new people. Plus, it was a time to test and challenge everything, including themselves.

Like any other business that employs people on a temporary basis, stories can become urban legends. Santa's Village is no exception. Stories of the park have been handed down from summer to summer and from year to year. Some are based on truth, some happened at other theme parks, and some are just fabricated tales. Most stories have been embellished in one way or another.

Santa's Village officially closed in 2006. What the long-term future holds for the property remains to be seen. What is constant though, is that for over 20 million visitors to the park there are some fond memories of the rides, shows, and attractions. Santa's Village was a Chicago-area icon and is still Dundee's most noted landmark.

For some of the former 11,000 summertime employees, Santa's Village holds some unique memories and some lifelong friendships and behind-the-scene stories that are all their own. For others, Santa's Village was a time to learn, grow, and even pull a prank or two. Either way, Santa's Village was a rite of summer that will not be forgotten.

Phillip L. Wenz
September 2010

Note: The stories contained in this book are of the opinion of the people and/or persons who submitted the writings to the author of the book, Christopher Dearman. Mr. Wenz was asked to provide his own stories and opinions as well as provide historical information. The sole responsibility of the content and context of this book lies completely with Christopher Dearman.

# ✪ PROLOGUE ✪

Prowling back and forth on an elevated platform in front of half a dozen DayGlo painted garbage cans that are annoyingly opening and closing hydraulically behind me, I stand with microphone in hand, imploring a bunch of pasty-faced tourists to pony up a buck to make fools of themselves. It's the Saturday of Memorial Day weekend, traditionally one of the park's busiest, and my Tin Can Alley game partner Ryan and I already have the game operating at full capacity, even though the gates opened less than an hour ago.

The Games manager, being astute enough to put his two most microphone-skilled employees on the popular game this extremely busy day, was standing off to the side with a sly grin on his face. As he watched the two of us taking turns playing circus barker for minimum wage, I imagine he was mentally calculating how much longer it would take before we made the park a historic profit. From the looks of all the eager, out-of-shape, cotton candy eating fools digging in their jean-shorts pockets trying to scrounge up the dollar to play—we would easily break all records before the end of the day.

Seeing all the customers congregated on the black pavement in front of me, waiting for the chance to hurl as many armfuls of plastic colored balls as possible towards the intermittently slamming trash can lids—my boss wasn't the only one with a sly grin on his face. While patrons were spending money hand over fist, trying to win a cheap stuffed animal that cost about a nickel to produce, I was mentally counting out my own historic profit that was taking place on this hot summer day. Unbeknownst to everyone around me, there was easily over a hundred pilfered dollars jammed into my blue polyester shorts pocket—and it wasn't even noon yet…

# CHAPTER ONE

# SANTA'S VILLAGE

# ✪ SANTA'S VILLAGE ✪
## DUNDEE, ILLINOIS
### - A HISTORICAL OVERVIEW -
### BY PHILLIP L. WENZ

Santa's Village was born of a man, who as a child had no real Christmas. Glenn Holland grew up in California during the Great Depression. His parents died by the time he was 18 years old, leaving him to care for his younger sister. As a grown man, Holland married and had children. As a father, he tried to give his own children the type of Christmas that he only knew in his dreams.

In the early 1950's, struck with inspiration, Holland sat at his kitchen table one day and started to sketch his idea of a Christmas fairyland where all the magic of the holiday would come to life. Holland developed this idea into a working plan and began finding investors for his project. He traveled the country selling his "Santa's Village" concept, and eventually listed his new company, "Santa's Village Corporation," on the California Stock Exchange.

The first Santa's Village opened in 1955, six weeks before Disney-land, in Skyforest near Lake Arrowhead in San Bernardino County, California (closed 1998). A second Santa's Village opened in 1957 near Scotts Valley in Santa Cruz County, California (closed 1979).

With the success of the first and second Santa's Villages, Holland began scouting a third location in the Midwest. The Chicago area, home to two Worlds' Fairs, birthplace of the Ferris Wheel, and a center of entertainment and culture was picked as the spot. A suburban location, approximately 45 miles northwest of the city, was chosen.

Dundee, Illinois was a tiny little town with some local attractions and a few good restaurants. The community was surrounded by cornfields and a huge forest wildlife foundation area. The newly-completed Northwest Tollway connected the small suburb to Chicago to the east and Rockford, Illinois to the west.

In April 1958, Holland entered into a fifty year land lease on forty wooded acres of McGraw's Wildlife Foundation with Chicago businessman Edwin Eichier. The property, located on State Routes 25 and 72, was similar to the settings of Holland's two California endeavors. In September, ground was broken and the third Santa's Village was born.

Santa's Village Corporation and general contractor Putnam Henck built Santa's Village Dundee, Illinois, in nine months at the cost of one million dollars. The Dundee park officially opened on Memorial Day weekend in 1959 to large crowds. On hand to greet these visitors of all ages was Santa, Mrs. Claus, and numer-ous helpers dressed as pixies and elves. These pixies and elves operated rides, worked in shops, and served food to the public. Santa had a petting zoo with sheep, ducks, goats, and Penny Peck, the educated chicken. Children could ride a Mexican burro or in a sleigh, pulled by real live reindeer from Unalakeet, Alaska. Other rides included a giant whirling Christmas Tree, gasoline-powered tractors, and the Tree House Slide. Children could see a puppet show at the Wee Puppet Theatre. A giant Jack-in-the-Box, and brightly colored mushrooms dotted the landscape.

There was also Santa's Post Office, Reindeer Barn, and a Gingerbread House. Mrs. Claus made fresh candy daily in her Candy Kitchen. The Pixie Pantry served hotdogs, hamburgers, fries, and sodas. Santa's Toy Factory was also there by the magic pond. Wishing wells, toy soldiers, and outdoor displays could be seen. Music flowed from treetop speakers. There was even an egg-shaped hut for the Easter Bunny. As you looked around the Village, you could see over a dozen log buildings, stores, and attractions. These buildings had pointed roofs, strengthened by rafters. The log structures were brightly colored and had wonderful detail like gingerbread trim and surrealist features. They fit into the beautiful trees that are part of the Fox Valley region.

Santa's Village, in the first few seasons, was open 364 days a year. The layout of the "Village" stayed pretty much the same until an extensive expansion program, which began in early 1962, started to change the makeup of the park.

Arrow Development of California was contracted by Santa's Village Corporation to develop some new attractions for the park. Arrow was best known at the time as the company that built the Disneyland rides in Anaheim, California. The first major change came in the removal of the wishing well in the front of the park next to the Entrance House.

Ground was broken in the spring of 1962 for the Dundee Village's most enduring attraction...The Snowball Ride. Advertised as the original Snowball Ride, it was actually one of two Snowball Rides built. That same year the Scotts Valley Santa's Village in northern California also had one installed. The expansion also included the redevelopment of the Magic Train, which was relocated deeper into the forest setting of Santa's Village. A brand-new C.P. Huntington engine was added along with an extension of the tracks. The new layout actually looped in and out of the parking lot. The Antique Car Ride was installed in the space vacated by the Magic Train.

The year 1962 also saw the start of the biggest development in Santa's Village's history, The Polar Dome Ice Arena. The Polar Dome project was a major undertaking for Santa's Village Corporation. Part of the park's original layout had to be moved to make room for the 40,000 square foot ice arena. The first relocation was that of North Pole Plaza and Santa's House. They were moved into an empty space near the newly added Snowball Ride. Originally these two attractions sat near where center ice of the dome is today. They also relocated the Toy Soldier (Duck Pond) and the Jack-in-the-Box Snow Cone Stand. The Polar Dome project took a little more than a year to complete at the cost of $350,000, a very tidy sum in the early 1960's.

The dome opened in February 1963 to national reviews. The original Polar Dome Ice Arena design sat 4,000 people and was the largest air-supported dome stadium in the world, according to *The Guinness World Book of Records*. Top name acts appeared in the dome, such as the International Showtime Circus with Don Ameche. Magician Mark Wilson's Magic Land of Allakazam was presented and filmed in the dome for national audiences. Major sports like the National Olympic Speed Skating Competition (videotaped for ABC's Wide World of Sports), and the Chicago Blackhawks practice sessions and exhibition games were held. Numerous ice skating revues, hockey leagues, wrestling matches, concerts, and roller derby events filled out the entertainment.

Santa's Village was also a big hit in the movies. Between 1964 and 1966 three movie "shorts" were shot on location in the park by Florida-based producer K. Gordon Murray (1964's *Santa Claus and His Helpers*, 1966's *Santa's Magic Kingdom*, and 1966's *Santa's Enchanted Village*). The featurettes used the park's employees and characters in the cast as well as some of the Village's more noticeable props. These one-reel movies have not only been seen in the United States but also in Great Britain, France, and Mexico.

With all the expansion that Santa's Village Corporation was having in Illinois, Holland miscalculated the park's operating season. The two California Santa's Villages could operate 364 days a year. The Dundee park started out that way, but the Chicago area weather was so unbearable and unpredictable during the winter months that attendance was low. Santa's Village in Dundee was being put in the odd position of being closed at Christmas. Financial problems ensued.

The year 1965 saw the end of Santa's Village Corporation in Illinois. Glenn Holland sold the park and its Illinois assets to Adventureland owner Durell Everding, closing the chapter on the original owner of Santa's Village in Dundee, Illinois.

During the Everding era, Santa's Village continued to adapt and grow. The facility could operate year-round, but not simultaneously. Santa's Village would now open on Mother's Day in May and close the last weekend of October. The Polar Dome Ice Arena would open in September and close in April. Everding also had a plan of adding new rides that would attract older children, thus making the park a total family experience. It worked.

Sadly the "heydays" of the Polar Dome ended when a storm raced through the Dundee area in 1966, tearing open the skin of the inflatable dome and laying it across the inside of Santa's Village. The dome went through a major overhaul and remodeling. A flat roof was added a year later.

The early-1970's saw the passing of Durell Everding. A group of gentlemen known as the Medina Investors purchased the park. Barney Clark, the principal of the group, kept the park in the same direction as that of Everding. To help "sell" this new and improved version of the park, the name was changed to the "Three Worlds of Fun Theme Park." The "Three Worlds" were Santa's World, the original area of the park; Old McDonald's Farm, which replaced the reindeer barn area, and the Coney Island section of larger rides and games of skill. The name, "Three Worlds of Fun," never really caught on. Plus, another theme park in Kansas City, Missouri had a similar name. To avoid confusion, Management added Santa's Village to the name again, thus becoming, "The Three Worlds of Santa's Village."

The tenure of the Medina Investors was relatively short, as in 1978 the park was once again on the market for sale.

The year of 1978 saw two McHenry County businessmen take over the park. The North Pole Corporation had some new and bold ideas. They added a water and action park, Racing Rapids. The water park was one of the first such parks in the Midwest, and the largest in the state of Illinois when it opened in 1983.

The late 1980's into the early 1990's saw new growth in record attendance and in the addition of new and exciting attractions. Rides like the Galaxy Roller Coaster, the Balloon Race, and the YO-YO were opened. Outdoor shows and new eating facilities dotted the park's landscape. The late 1990's saw the addition of the park's first looping coaster, the Typhoon.

In 2003, the name of the park was shortened from "The Three Worlds of Santa's Village" back to "Santa's Village Theme Park." Under the management of North Pole Corporation, the park headed into the 21st century and into a milestone.

May of 2004 saw Santa's Village hit 45 years of family fun. Very few theme parks achieve this milestone, thus becoming a park of five generations of visitors. Santa's Village provided a way for children to experience some of the same attractions that their parents experienced as children.

At the close of the 2004 season, Sterling Bay Companies, a Chicago-based real estate development firm, purchased the land on which Santa's Village sits. Rumors were spreading that Santa's Village would not re-open. On Mother's Day 2005 the park opened as usual. It would become Santa's Village's 46th and last season.

2005 also saw a group of Dundee businessmen calling themselves "North Pole Village, L.L.C." approaching North Pole Corporation to buy the assets of Santa's Village along with the land that the park sits upon. The land lease held by North Pole Corporation was set to expire in March of 2008. If this deal was successful, North Pole Village, L.L.C. would have put Santa's Village assets and land together for the first time in history. In June of 2006 the deal was in default.

In August of 2006 judgements against both North Pole Corporation and North Pole Village, L.L.C. were handed down by the Kane County Circuit Court. Both companies were evicted from the park property. Long time owner North Pole Corporation held an auction in October of 2006 of the non-fixed assets. The infra-structure stayed in place. Sterling Bay Companies are keeping their options open as to the future of Santa's Village. In January of 2007, the property was listed for sale and was closed to the public.

Since 2007, an attempt to open a new Santa's Village in downstate Utica has seen some promise at the Grand Bear Lodge. In 2010, the property in Dundee was renamed "Santa's Village Expo" by the Sterling Bay Companies in an attempt to re-open parts of the park. And what does the future have in store for Santa's Village? It is hard to say...but one thing is for certain, Santa's Village has entertained five generations of visitors, has become a Chicagoland tradition, and remained true to its origins and family orientation.

# ✪ SANTA'S VILLAGE MEMORIES ✪

*"Where else could you goof off,
get a tan, make lifelong friends -
and get paid for it!"*

- Former Santa's Village Employee

**G**eorge Strissel worked for the North Pole Corporation from **1989 through 1993 in the Games & Rides Departments, as well as working as a skate guard at the Polar Dome:** *"The overall experience of being able to work outside all summer long was awesome. It was a great time working with a bunch of high school and college kids—looking to earn a little money, and party a lot during the summer months. It was always a good time during and after the softball games between departments, and I met a lot of people that became great friends—as well as getting great farmer tans!*

**J**ennifer Miller-Riggs worked the Roller Bowler game during the summer of 1991. She used to spend Mother's Days at Santa's Village with her mother, and got one chance to do so

11

with her own kids before the park closed: *"I still remember the smell when you walked in...the sticky food-crusted black top that led up to the ice pole in front of the Snowball ride. There isn't a part of that place that I don't remember...we went every year of my childhood."*

# DON'T NEED NOTHING BUT A ...

**A**former Games & Guest Relations worker from the 80's recalls a few fond memories: *"I remember pitching nickels on the dome roof in hopes that it would rain and the park would close. I've met many lifetime friends working there. Believe it or not, working there taught me my work ethic. I loved the Maintenance parties; they used the money from the magic pond and threw one hell of a good time!"*

**A**fter spending a few hours trying to recall his time working at Santa's Village, one former Rides employee summed up his memories with this: *"Damn, we had a good time back then!"*

**M**eghan Williams, whose last name was Earsley when she worked in the gift shops during the summer of 1994, never had any "gone wild" moments while working due to fearing the bosses. But, she remembers that every employee got a little crazy on the last day of the season. She has many good time memories of her days there: *"I worked with a bunch of my friends, and was able to meet many more while there that season. I have tons of memories from working at Santa's Village, but I would have to say the best came from when I helped out in the picnic area. I worked the gate with others. It was always a blast. Depending on what kind of group was coming in, you always got free things from them, from hats to anything else like that."*

*"I remember working the day the FOP\* had its company picnic. There were so many police officers. Some got rowdy, but it was the best time. One of the other best times I had was when I would end up getting off work early. I would go change out of my uniform, and I would go on the rides with other employees. Since I worked in the Shops Department, I always got stuck working the gift booth down in Coney Island, right next to the bumper cars. I always knew some of the words to the Beach Boy songs because of my mom, but working that booth caused me to know every word to every song. Now, I hate hearing the Beach Boys at times!"*

*"It was a great experience working at Santa's Village. I met so many new people. It was my first real job, and I would change nothing about it. I was sad to see it go, but the memories of the many years I went there, and the summer I worked there, will live on forever!!!!"*

You couldn't ask for a better
first job - there was just
so many good times!
- Former Santa's Village Employee

**J**anice Larson worked at Santa's Village from the summer of 1973 through the summer of 1976 while attending college. She worked the concession stands for two years, was a waitress in the Polar Dome restaurant for one, and was the co-manager of the Pixie Pantry her last season: *"I had worked the*

---

\* FOP - Stands for the Fraternal Order of Police, who had many annual picnics at the park over the years that were enjoyed by thousands of cops, and dreaded by just as many employees.

*previous summer for the Park District at the swimming pools, but a lot of my friends worked at Santa's Village and they seemed to be having a lot of fun doing it—not to mention meeting some pretty hot guys!"*

*"I have a lot of wonderful memories about Santa's Village. It basically was the cornerstone of my social life for the four years I worked there, and I kept in close touch with many of the kids I worked with for years. In fact, I just flew to Memphis with three of my girlfriends last fall to visit another Santa's Village buddy we worked with who is battling a serious illness."*

# FUN WITH MAGIC MUSHROOMS

**A** Games employee recalls fondly the simple pleasures that some of the large mushrooms in front of the park provided while waiting for rides home. *"After watching the fantastic time being had by kids sliding down the mushrooms, I couldn't resist giving it a go myself. I have to say—I had a BLAST doing it!"*

**P**hil Wenz, who played Santa at the park for twenty years, sheds some light on the famous fungi: *"The park has a few different iconic things. The North Pole probably is the most iconic, but the mushrooms are right there. Originally, there was probably about three dozen of them in the park—today there's maybe eighteen or nineteen. They are these huge concrete structures. Take the height of the mushroom, and there is that much cement underneath the ground—those things aren't moving. We had a guy try to steal one of the front mushrooms not too long ago. He put a chain around one; then hooked it to the bumper of his car. Sure enough, we come out one morning to find an old bumper laying in the parking lot!"*

# LIFE PRESERVERS OPTIONAL

**K**aren L. DeBias spent summers in the blazing heat working for $1.25/hour in 1974, 1975 & 1976. She worked in
**Rides, Games & Food Service, and submitted in her words some
"very tame" stories:** *"I met my very 'first love' at Santa's Village! In
fact, there was a group of us 'gals' from Dundee High School that all
worked at Santa's Village at the time. On a regular basis, we got together
weekly after-hours with the 'guys' we met at Santa's Village from other
high schools for softball games, parties, and frequent trips to Adventure
Land!"*

**She'll never forget when...** *"I was working the other side of the
'dock' on the paddleboat ride. There were always two sets of two ride
operators working the paddleboat rides. The side that I was NOT on
had loaded the paddleboat, but neglected to estimate the anticipated
weight of the paddleboat! Needless to say, when I turned around after
I had loaded my paddleboat—I was shocked to see the paddleboat on
the other side of the dock was 'going down'! YIKES! What a day!"*

**C**hristopher French recalls a summer back in the late 70's
when he had to dress up in one of the Three Bears cos-
**tumes that were used by many:** *"One big fella even gave all of us
mono towards the end of the summer! I worked at Santa's Village the
summer of either '78 or '79. I sang and danced in the disco-type variety*

show three times per day in the Polar Dome. I also was required to go out into the park several times a day and be a part of the Goldilocks and the Three Bears singing sensation."

**Being that the costumes had to be shared during the blistering heat, things unfortunately got rather sweaty...** *"As I mentioned before, this required sharing one of the bear suits with two other sweaty men. I'm certain that is how I contracted mononucleosis! Still had some great memories of the place, though."*

**But some of his memories weren't always the greatest...** *"The talent level of this particular group of singers was unusually high. Quite honestly, while I make my living as a classical musician today, I am not, and have never been, a singer. Hey, I was hired and I needed the summer job...so I sang and danced. Frankly, I was horrible!"*

*"I have a horrible memory from that summer. The director of the show asked me if I wanted to sing a solo at one point during the summer. I wholeheartedly agreed that this would be fun. He gave me a tape of "Bless the Beasts and the Children" in which the melody was somehow softened, and the accompaniment was left at full volume. I'm absolutely certain this was a rudimentary technique even for the late 70's. I took the tape home, learned the words, practiced in front of the mirror, and begged my parents to come see me perform the next day."*

*"Dutifully, they came and sat through the corny disco crap until my big moment came. At this point the director inserted the cassette tape... but left the volume turned down too low. When I finally heard anything at all it was somewhere mid-tune. I had no earthly idea where in the song I was supposed to be. I wandered pitch-wise, sounding like a tone-deaf moron, all the while watching my parents sink lower and lower into their seats out of embarrassment. No one rescued me; I just aimlessly murmured for over four minutes. A real pro, I am."*

*"Afterward, I was too mortified to even laugh at myself. Everyone was kind, mostly. Obviously, I wasn't asked to sing another solo. A back-up singer/dancer, I would remain until the show mercifully closed at the end of the summer. If we're made stronger by our defeats, hell, I'm a real stud now!"*

> "Working my first job at Santa's Village went a long way in making me the person I am today"
> – Former Employee

# THE GOOD, THE BAD & THE...

An employee that wants to go by the name—"The Cotton Candy/Popcorn Lady" – worked at Santa's Village for her first official job from 1987-90 in the Foods Department. One of the perks was that she got to use the shredded employee food tickets as confetti at her high school Homecoming games. She remembers all the friendships she made, and the priceless memories. She has mostly good memories of those times: *"Having the boss slip $20's in my pocket on busy days, and eating Rambo's famous hot dogs from 3 Worlds. Having my best friend decorating the popcorn wagon to the hilt for my 16th birthday—I love her! It was also fun to have little kids try and say: Osh Kosh-B'Gosh-B'Gosh-B'Gosh-B'Gosh—before giving them their pretzel or impressing them with my rainbow Sno-Cone making abilities."*

**But there were also a couple bad ones...** *I recall burning my arm on a pizza oven at 3 Worlds, and the times I had to beg someone to come relieve me from the popcorn wagon to go to the bathroom. Too much buttery popcorn equals a messy belly!*

# SAY CHEESE

**S**hannon Jacobs **remembers her three years working at** Santa's Village: *"I worked in the T-shirt shop. I think it was called, 'Santa's Portraits'? We had some crazy people in there. We put really awful pictures of people on t-shirts and calendars! People would pay for that! Ha! I had a blast, though! Easiest job I ever had."*

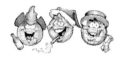

**A**nn Fox's **first job was working in Food Services when she was fifteen years old in the mid-1980's. She remembers the crazy food fights after-hours, and meeting her first boyfriend while he was sweeping the grounds:** *"I don't remember anything much else except we raised a lot of hell! We were young, and there were never really any supervisors. I remember that the concession stands were always pretty filthy, and we would take off early to ride the rides."*

*"I know we liked to hang out on the giant mushrooms, but my friends there and I were pretty good kids. We didn't drink or do drugs. I got my first kiss there though from the guy I met, and then later dated all through college. He took me to prom, and then to my debutante ball through Marmion."*

*"I know it is not very exciting, but I remember it to be a good summer full of great friends, and was a very cool first job to have."*

# SANTA WASN'T THE ONLY CELEBRITY TO ROAM THE PARK

**J**ay Cramer worked at the park for four seasons in the Games Department—where he never stole a dime, as a Grounds manager—where he hated every second of it, and at the Polar Dome snack bar—where he loved eating pizza puffs. He ended up quitting because he hated working for one of his supervisors, but seeing one unique sight while working still sticks in his mind: *"Geena Davis was visiting the park while in town filming 'A League of Their Own'—she was freakishly tall!"*

**P**hil Wenz recalls some notable visitors as well: *Governor George Ryan, Governor James Edgar, Danny Bonaduce from the Partridge Family, Rich Koz from the Koz Zone, Bill Campbell from Chicagoing and Cookie the Clown from the Bozo Show!*

"I totally remember the General Manager Don—I always think of him when I see Mr. Burns on The Simpsons!"

-Former Santa's Village Employee

**M**arc Schock worked for two seasons in the Grounds crew during the summers of 1999 & 2000. His favorite memory is the friendships & bonds that were made while working:

*"There was one morning the second season working there, before the park opened, [when] the older crew leaders decided my 'trial by fire' was completed, and decided to commemorate the occasion by throwing me in the crocodile pond by the windmill for a little dip in my work clothes. It was funny and refreshing!"*

*"Growing up almost right behind Santa's Village, you could hear the siren song of the Fire Truck ride all summer long. After the Typhoon roller coaster was built, it became the screams of mom, dad and children. I remember one summer in the late 70's when my family was out playing in the front of our house, and you could hear this rumble coming down the hill like a freight train. It was all the horses—from the ponies to the Clydesdales—stampeding towards us. Some had stopped for a quick bite to eat of our lawn, and others continued down the hill towards Duncan Ave. Almost every summer growing up, my family had made a visit to Santa's Village, and eventually I got to take my own son there one last time before the closing season. As run-down as it was becoming, it was still full of those childhood memories, and I even had to stop and recall those wild summers as a teenager at Santa's Village."*

**C**hris Morgan, who helped run the Ice Cream Shop from 1988 to 1990, felt lucky to work in one of the few places in the park that had air conditioning, as well as a window with a great view of the Evergreen Stage next door (where he also witnessed frisky employees getting busy from time to time). He remembers passing the time by playing hockey in the back room with a sanitizer cap & two brooms, along with many other stories of the time spent during those hot summer months:

*"My full-time summer career at Santa's Village started at age 13. At the time, my parents were having trouble with their marriage, so to get out of the house I forged a birth certificate with an old Royal typewriter! I used white out, a pencil and a copy machine at Ben Franklin in East Dundee. The work permit was issued off of the forgery by the private school I attended."*

*"My starting wage was $2.90 an hour even though minimum wage was much higher at the time. The Food Service Department was set up as a catering company for tax purposes. The staff was paid server wages, but we were not allowed to collect tips!"*

*"They made me the manager of the ice cream shop, and I was in charge of inventory, deliveries, and the cash register. One day I got tired of working for so little, so I convinced the owner to pay me $20.00 extra on each check in cash, or I would quit. My check was the only one distributed in a white envelope. If you are keeping score, this 'raise' netted out to be an additional .50 cents an hour—I sure showed them."*

**The job did have its perks…** *"My day consisted of parking my ten-speed in back, and opening the shop. Most days we blasted Great White, Vanilla Ice and Guns & Roses on a boom box near the register. I was always creeped out by the dipping well freezer though, because they used it in the winter to store dead deer from hunting. I was not a hunter, so every time I dipped the dipper in to get a scoop of ice cream I would envision deer eyes looking back at me! A mint chocolate chip shake at 9:00 am usually made me forget the freezer for a while."*

**But the owner usually frowned on the practice of free desserts...** *"Santa came in one day and it had to be over a hundred outside. Add twenty degrees with a full beard and velvet suit—needless to say, Santa was thirsty. He did not have his wallet on him, and was unable to produce any of the blue meal tickets issued to the staff at a reduced rate. Having empathy for him, and not wanting to cause a scene by refusing Santa service at his own village, I gave him a black cow for free. I can see in his eyes this is probably the kindest thing I could have done all summer. The owner of the shop, Mr. Hankie, was standing by the doorway and witnessed me providing free product to an employee, and gave me an earful. All I recall is him sarcastically asking me if Santa was my mother! I replied 'no,' and he proceeded to brutally explain that 'employees do not get free meals policy' to me. The village was named after this man, and it would have been pretty awkward refusing service in his own home. Mr. Hankie died shortly after that incident. I am pretty sure it was from a heart attack—no foul play was suspected."*

**Maybe it was due to the fumes?** *"The ice cream shop constantly smelled like a swimming pool. We could never find the cause of the mystery smell, so we used triple the bleach on rags to cover up the odor. Eventually we found the cause. There was a drip pan that was not changed for two years! Nobody knew it existed until a repair man pointed it out to us."*

**Final thoughts?** *"I served thousands of happy kids and families ice cream and learned much about the value of work, dealing with crowds, and creating the Disney experience. Santa's Village to me was an important part of my childhood...even if I only made three dollars an hour!"*

# SMELLY CAT, SMELLY CAT
# IT'S NOT YOUR FAULT...

**O**ne former employee recalls the summer he worked in an **unbearably hot costume:** *Working as the fucking Coney Cat was hell on earth! I spent day after day in the blazing heat in that silly costume—it was miserable!"*

### "I once kicked Coney Kitty in the ass!"

#### -Anonymous Former Employee

**P**hil Wenz remembers the days of the Coney Cat as well: *"That Coney Island Kitty and other mascots could be disgusting, if they were not taken care of! The kids for the characters used to get into the costumes right by my dressing room where they had an area partitioned off, and it got to the point where I would walk through where they kept the heads and such, and the smell—my god—they never thought about taking those things to the cleaners! One day one of the managers comes up there and sees all the animals were gone—the heads, the bodies, everything. So he knocks on my door—where are all the costumes at? I looked him in the eye and said—I took them to the damn cleaners! I mean, I had to walk through all that stench daily, and I'm like, you got to clean these things! He tells me it was on his list of things to do, and I tell him not to worry about it—here's the receipt, and now you just have to go pay and pick them up! Boy, he was pissed when he got the bill, but my response to that was—would YOU wear it?"*

# WHOEVER SMELT IT, DEALT IT

**J**ohn McMillion has a confession to make: *"A fellow co-worker named Luis and I were allowed to hang out in Santa's House on our breaks during one of the hot days. It was so nice and cool inside, and a great place to get out of the heat while Santa greeted kids. One time while it was really crowded in the house during our lunch break, I accidentally let a fart slip. My god, it was an awful smell! We left the house quickly, leaving poor Santa, moms, and children to sit with the lingering smell. I never admitted to Luis or anyone else it was me—until now!"*

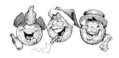

# DID YOU AT LEAST GET ANY ICE CREAM?

**T**ania Binning worked in the Games Department in the mid-nineties when she was fifteen: *"I'd say my best memories of working there are trying to dodge the spitting llama when it was our shift to clean the parking lot and take it to the dumpsters. We'd always try to get the boys to do it, but they thought it was funny to watch us scream and run.*

**Loogie-hacking animals weren't the only cause for her screaming...** *"Getting locked in the skeeball closet one day because my co-worker thought I went down to change some money in. The music was* *always pretty loud in there, so she couldn't hear me knocking on the door and yelling her name. I had to wait until someone won a prize for her to open the door again. I was probably stuck for a good 15-20 minutes!"*

# WELL IT DID HAVE THE NICKNAME, "SATAN'S VILLAGE"*

**W**hile almost everyone had his or her times of stress, one Games employee made the most of it: *"My first day working there they had a bunch of us out in the picnic grove, cleaning up garbage! While the task itself was degrading, one kid decided to make things more bearable and snuck in his boom-box to listen to some tunes. We were jamming out to music from the 80's hair-band Extreme with no supervision. A stupid memory, but one for some reason it gives me a smile—which can't always be said about picking up trash!"*

**A**nother Games employee's memories were not quite as fond: *"I remember when we had to pick up the dirty parking lot, all the dirty diapers and garbage. Walking the parking lot...it was horrible—what a terrible job!"*

**S**ome took to letting Mother Nature be their savior: *"You always prayed for thunderstorms for two reasons. One, it was hot as hell more often than not, and two, they would shut the park down and you got to go home early!"*

**H**e wasn't the only one who had had complaints: *"I just remember how hot it was all the time—never getting breaks —*

---

\* SATAN'S VILLAGE - along with the more friendly - The Village or The Park were slang names given to Santa's Village by its employees.

which there was no rhyme or reason to any of it. When someone decided to show up to give you a break, that's when you had it. There was no set breaks or anything you could depend on."

**S**ome still have nightmares: *"To this day I still sometimes flash back to how absolutely disgusting some of those bathrooms got on the extreme busy days. Dirty diapers just thrown about, piss all over the floors, rotting food and sweat-filled paper towels overflowing from trash bins—I just puked in my mouth thinking about it!"*

# CHAPTER TWO

# SANTA & THE
# NORTH POLE

# PHIL WENZ INTERVIEW

**S**o tell me a little about your time spent working as the longest tenured Santa at Santa's Village.

*"Probably one of the best places to work in the park! I could come and go as I pleased. In those days my life pretty much revolved around the Santa's House. It literally was almost an around-the-clock job, so as long as I showed up, I was pretty much left alone. Santa was my business."*

**How was it spending your days, cooped up in Santa's House?**

*"It was fantastic! I had full say on how the house was furnished and equipped. I like comfort, and if I was going to be there—I was going to be comfortable! It had a stocked fridge filled with sodas, cookies and snacks. We had a little television in there so we got to watch the Bears on Sunday, and also a radio to listen to the Cubs or White Sox games. The beauty was that it was set up so that the helpers could turn everything off with a click of a button when we had visitors."*

*"The way the house was set up, I could pretty much see who was coming from any angle, so if we saw someone coming, I'd give the signal, and then everything would be back to Christmas. It was also a great place to hide out for some of the upper management too. Phil Oestreich would sometimes come in there for 10-15 minutes at a time just to get away from everybody."*

**Sounds like a good gig. Anything ever get you annoyed?**

*"Yeah, I'd get annoyed when the air-conditioning would go out. The thing about that is the windows in Santa's House opened, but they had been painted over so many times that you really couldn't get them open. So there were times when the air-conditioning would go down, but you can't close Santa's House—you really couldn't do that—so we would have to improvise. I'd end up spending a lot of time out in the park on those days."*

*"Speaking of air-conditioning, one interesting fact is that Santa's House originally didn't have any from 1959 to 1963—so those four years I imagine Santa would sweat his butt off. That's why he stood outside Santa's House so much. He would greet the guests; then just have them walk through the house to view it."*

*"By the time I got there though, they had a really good air-conditioner in there. I told my helpers to make sure they dressed warm, because I'm going to keep this house as cold as possible! During hot days people would come in Santa's House, it smelled good from the 'cookie' air freshener we used, and the Christmas lights were flashing... people didn't want to leave!"*

*"Speaking of not wanting to leave, there was a time when a mom and*

dad brought their child in and said that they'd be back to pick him up in an hour and a half. I don't know what they were thinking! I guess they planned to go on some of the adult rides or something, and I'm like—this isn't going work here, folks."

## How did you spend your breaks when playing Santa?

"On lunch breaks I would either hang out in the office, or set an alarm in my dressing room and just take a nap. I didn't really eat any food while working."

## Any other funny situations occur on your watch?

"There would be times when people would come by and tell their kids—Santa is going to take you on the rides. Either that or people would come in complaining—you know your roller coaster is broke—and I'm like, let's think about this for a minute, you know it's not my rollercoaster!"

"Then we had a lady that came in, literally put her child down on the carpeted floor—then started to change his diapers! I was like no, no, no—we have bathrooms for that! It was WAY too small of a place to have that odor stuck in there. You're not changing him in Santa's House with all these people around! Stuff like that would happen more than you would think."

## Can you think of anything you witnessed that was weird?

"Seeing yourself on a billboard is sort of weird. I mean, I'm six feet tall, and I would see a six-foot tall picture of myself as I'm going to work while driving down the expressway!"

*"Another thing weird is how the years sort of blended together. Like when I looked at your Facebook picture—I remembered you, but I couldn't place exactly when. You just meet so many people at different times. What's odd about that is that there are a lot of people who don't know me as Phil—they know me as Santa. I could walk up to them out of costume, and they would have no idea who I was!"*

### Anything make you sad?

*"We had a couple instances where children would say—I don't want daddy to hit me with a belt—or stuff like that. Seeing abuse on some of these kids definitely bothered me. I've seen kids with black and blue marks and they would tell me that they fell down or fell off their bike— but you know what was happening."*

*"The helpers were trained what to do when we came across these situations. I could never ask a child's name because I was Santa, and I'm supposed to know these things, so the helpers would step in. They would have the kids sign their name in the Good Book—a little trick of the trade. Either that, or if I ever said—what's your name—that was a code that something was wrong. We then would make a decision and inform the park's management, if needed."*

### Speaking of Santa's Helpers, did anyone try hitting on the girls?

*"Not from the customers. But, one year one of the guys working the Duck Pond had a crush on one of them, and it really creeped her out. I was like a big brother to them though, so if there was a problem— we'd take care of it by discussing it with the personnel office"*

"They had a pretty nice gig. They got to take an hour lunch as I did, where all the other employees only got a half hour. They also got to leave right at park's close, and they didn't have to clean anything—I did all that. All they had to do is keep my daily sheets of how many pictures we took, and help make things run smoothly. They all were pretty good. I never really had any bad helpers. Just treat them with respect; let them know what the job is all about, and make sure you thank them. I appreciated the work they did."

### So did any women try hitting on Santa himself?

"No, I kept things on the up and up, but I did see some interesting things—especially in the summertime when women would come in the house in their bikini tops from the water park. When that happened, and they wanted to take a picture with Santa, you had to make sure that their hands were in a position were they covered themselves or put on a t-shirt. We had to be very conscious of what we allowed in pictures, because those things would get around. If someone came in with something on a shirt that we felt was inappropriate, or was wearing revealing clothing, we would make the person put on a sweatshirt that we had ready for those instances. I was working in parades and stuff outside the park. If something got out to the public that wasn't 'Santa appropriate'—it was my issue and it reflected on more than just the park. It is my livelihood."

### What is your happiest memory of working at the park?

"The day I brought Don Goers out—seeing him go back to the place he worked at for so many years. He had left in 1979, and hadn't been back to the park until I took him there in 1994. What happened was I ran into him at Spring Hill Mall when I was playing Santa out there, and *a friendship started up after talking with him. So I arranged to bring him back to work there for one day, and it was really neat. I just sat back and watched him work in the Santa suit one last time at the park. The sad thing about Don was that he never got any recognition or any publicity when he retired. He just sort of moved on after all those years. So it was cool to see him just jump right back into it, and get to be Santa there for one more day."*

**Speaking of the Santa Suit, tell me about yours. Did you ever have a child take a leak on you while wearing it?**

*"I've come pretty close to getting peed on, but when I see a kid making that face that he's about to go—he's immediately going to be passed back to the parents and getting off me!"*

*"As far as the suit, over my lifetime I've probably had about thirty to thirty-five of them, but it took me until 2004 before I realized I could get away with wearing just a vest rather then the full hot Santa jacket. I have twelve outfits now, including summer wear, and the older I get, the more the costumes change—different designer beards and whatnot. Heck, I might eventually even end up growing a real full Santa's beard someday."*

**Did you ever witness any tomfoolery while working at the park?**

*"Being we were pretty land locked in the house, we didn't really get to see much of the outside world. About the only thing that comes to mind is the one day back in 1992 when we were sitting there, and all of a sudden all the lights in the house went off. I go around back to see what happened, and of course I see some kids running away from the elec-*

trical box. So the next day I'm out there with a drill and padlock, and Don comes out and is like—what are you doing? I tell him I think we need a padlock on this. The park has been open for thirty-some years at that point and this thing doesn't have a padlock. No one ever thought about that—which was true for everyone. Nobody really noticed that box and it was just something no one thought about from day one."

**Any day at the park that really stands out?**

"I remember one weird day in 1990 or '91 when Management closed down the park gate because the park was just too crowded. It was a beautiful day. The attendance was right at fifteen thousand or so, which was a lot of people, and people could not move. We couldn't even get out of Santa's House! I'd look out the back door, and the line of people for the Snowball ride went all the way down the pathway. It was easily over a two-hour wait to see Santa. That day, when the park opened at ten, they let the gates open and we just saw a mass of people come flooding in and it was just nuts. I never saw anything like it in my life."

**Why did you choose not to be on the cover of your own book: *Images of America – Santa's Village*?**

"I wanted to show history. It's a throwback picture of Santa from 1963 and it just looked pretty neat. The story of the picture is that we were cleaning out upstairs, and at this point I had yet to come up with a picture to use for the cover. The publishers wanted me to suggest four or five different things—like a picture of the Christmas Tree ride or the Snowball ride, but some of the older pictures didn't seem to fit. They just didn't look right. So one day I was up in the office moving some boxes, and I see this old pile of papers. I started going through them, and the picture of Santa was embedded in the pile. I saw it, and that was it—that's the cover. I never saw it before; didn't even knew it had existed. It had to be lying face down in those papers for years. Those papers were dated like 1962 or 1963 so they had been lying there a long time."

"That was the beauty of going through old things like that; you just got to see so much history. After I started working at Santa's Village, I really started digging into the park's history, and all the different things that went on over the years. Since I was Santa, I was supposed to have been at the park since 1959, and was expected to know everything that had gone on since the park's opening. Throughout the years I found a wealth of material. Even after the park closed, I would come across memorabilia that had been hidden in little unused rooms and attics for years. I even found the actual blueprints that the foreman used to build the park. I found them in a crawlspace. They had to just be sitting there for decades since the park opened."

**Did you find anything else cool after the park closed?**

"There was actually a time capsule buried out in front of the park by the little house near the Santa's Village sign on Route 25. It was put there when the park opened in 1959. I didn't know it existed until the late Putty Henck told me about it. Henck was the general contractor on the park in 1959. So, after the park was closed (and after they auctioned off everything), we went and found it. It contained historical memorabilia, pictures of the park and stuff like that—basically an overview of the whole park. A lot of the stuff in the box was preserved very well, and other stuff I'm still not sure what it is."

# ✪ THE NORTH POLE ✪

Ask people what they remember most about Santa's Village and more often than not they will mention the frozen North Pole. Eager kids, as well as adults, couldn't help but feel the icy stick standing in front of Santa's House that would stay cold even on the hottest of days. The North Pole has been felt, touched, rubbed, stroked, and yes, even licked by literally thousands. Santa Phil Wenz has many memories of what he describes as the iconic symbol and heart of the park:

*"There was only one North Pole over the years. There were many different sign toppers, but only one pole. During its time at the park, it was in three different locations. In 1959, it was in the center of the park at the North Pole Plaza. The first time it was moved—they moved it over by the Snowball—right smack dab in the middle of the walkway. I heard somebody had hit it with a car, so they eventually moved it next to Santa's House."*

*"There was this one time there was this big party, it had to be a FOP day. The park was extremely crowded, and they were basically running out*

*of ice—they just couldn't keep up! People were sweating all over, and it was just a real hot day. So I'm standing outside the house, and I see this one lady come over and take a nail file from her purse. She starts scraping the ice off into a glass of soda—and then she started drinking it! I'm standing there talking to kids, and I'm about just ready to gag! These kids had been rubbing up against it, wearing suntan lotion, and it didn't phase her—she wanted that ice!"*

*"There were only six North Poles in the whole world, all made by the same company. Three were made for the Santa's Village Corporation, one for each park. The town of North Pole, Colorado has one. North Pole, New York has one, and I believe the last one was in Ontario, Canada. I actually have the one from the Dundee park at my home! The company that originally made them went out of business a long time ago, and when the town of Santa Claus, Indiana wanted to have one, they tried to make it themselves, but couldn't get it right. They actually wanted to crack the one I have open to see how it was made! I wasn't taking that chance."*

*"How it worked was that there was this compressor next to Santa's House that would shoot Freon, and push it through the middle of the pole. There was a tube that went straight up the middle. The gas would hit the top and then cascade down to the bottom and cycle back. The core of the pole would be kept in the neighborhood of about 22 degrees, so when the air hit it, it would form condensation and freeze to it."*

*"Every morning I would go into the Polar Dome to get a bucket of hot water, and I would dump it over the pole. It would glaze over and clean it off. I would dig out anything that was embedded in there, because kids would stick pennies on it. It would start to freeze into a solid sheet of ice and about an hour and a half later it would form snow on the*

column. At 10 o'clock the park would open and the first kid would come over and start the whole tradition of touching the ice for the day.

"It really was the marquee of the park. Like I said, people would lick it; people would shave ice off into their coolers and I would find hair in there. I think it was just such a fixture of the place. When you came around that corner and saw the pole, it truly did give the place a little magic."

## OTHERS ALSO HAD MEMORIES OF THE NORTH POLE:

* "That glorious frozen germ bar that every sick child licked or groped!"

* "It was also our family's meeting place when we got separated, I liked to touch the ice so much that I would get lost on purpose!"

* "There were numerous times I would use that pole to cool off while working. Yeah, it was disgusting, if you really thought about it. But man it got so damn hot there sometimes. You would see this frozen oasis standing there, just begging to be rubbed up on!"

* "Peeing on the frozen pole! After the park closed one day (an employee) whipped out

his dick and made a pattern of yellow lines on the pole. He sprayed his piss wildly to make sure he covered all five feet of pole. It was disgusting because we did not need to see his dick again, and kids licked the ice off of the pole during the day!"

✱ "Yeah, I think pretty much every male employee either pissed on that thing, or at least thought about it!"

✱ "Awe man, don't tell me that–I used to love that thing!"

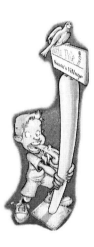

# Santa Don Goers

## By Phillip L. Wenz

To me there is only one Santa Claus that is really Santa from Santa's Village and that man is Don Goers. An Algonquin, Illinois native, Don first came to Santa's Village in 1959 as part of the Maintenance Department. He started to help out "Santa" that same year by playing the part to give a day off to the main Santa. He is among the original gentlemen who played the role at the park in 1959.

Goers made "Santa" his own in 1966, taking the role over full-time that year. As Santa, he invoked a jolly demeanor that was more a reflection of his personality, making him a natural for the character. His wide smile and hearty belly laugh were his trademark.

Spending twenty years at Santa's Village in the Maintenance Department, and then as Santa, Goers saw the park grow from just a few rides and attractions to the addition of the Polar Dome and the "Coney Island" section. Each year, tens of thousands of children visited him in Santa's House and throughout the park. Leaving the park in 1979, he returned only once to be Santa again. It would be in 1994 on the 35th anniversary year of the park.

I met Don Goers as a child many years before I was to become his successor. I would not meet him again until some twenty-seven years later during the Christmas of 1993 at Spring Hill Mall in West Dundee, Illinois. I was the opening day-shift Santa that year. Sometime during the course of that Christmas season while out shopping, Don and his wife came up to the Santa set at the mall and started to have a small conversation with the photo operation manager. After this conversation, Don came up and introduced himself to me. Of course hearing his name I knew exactly who he was.

We chatted for a minute and I asked if he would stick around a few minutes as my shift was about to end. He agreed. After I was out of costume, Don, his wife and I sat in my dressing room, talking about Santa and Santa's Village. We had a lot in common. The conversation lasted about an hour and then we exchanged phone numbers.

Spring of 1994 saw Santa's Village celebrate thirty-five years of being a landmark in the Northern Fox River Valley. As the park's season progressed, I thought it would be neat if I could have Don come back for a day and be Santa once again at Santa's Village. After a few phone calls between us, he agreed. June saw Santa Don Goers return to Santa's Village.

The day started off with me meeting Don in the main office. (It wasn't like he didn't know his way around.) From there I took him to the dressing room where he changed into his costume. When he walked out in full regalia as Santa, you could see a little smile beneath his moustache. Standing in front of me was the Santa that I knew as a child.

Santa Don and I went out of the dressing area and over to Santa's House. I opened the door for him and for the first time in fifteen years, Don was back "home" once again. He sat in Santa's chair and rapped his knuckles on the chair. It was of course the same chair that he and all who ever played the character had sat in.

I left Santa's House for a few minutes and, when I came back, I glanced in the window. It was a strange feeling peering into the house. There was Santa in his house, just as I remembered him as a child. Walking inside, I felt as if I had just traveled back in time.

Don Goers had changed himself into Santa Claus and he had changed me into a little boy once again. It was magic.

Don played Santa all day that day. A few newspapers came out to interview him. It was his day, but it was also my day. It is not too often that two people from different eras have a chance to interact and share some of the same experiences. Each of us got to go back in time for a brief moment. In age we are thirty-eight years apart, but in the Santa's Village world we share so much and the same role. We will always be connected by that common bond.

I still see Santa Don every now and then. I enjoy the conversations and enjoy the fact that we have the opportunity to talk about the park. Of all my days at Santa's Village, the day I got to "revisit" with Santa is by far my most cherished.

# HOLLY

## By Phillip L. Wenz

**J**ust a really good kid. I have one child and she is a wonderful young lady in her early twenties. Holly is part of not only my life and family, she is part of my Santa Claus world. As a child she came out to Santa's Village to see me and enjoyed the park. She knew that I "helped" Santa. When I did have a day off, I would take her around the park and enjoy Santa's Village just as any other parent would.

I often wonder how she felt about having a father that was basically Santa all the time. Other fathers were firemen, managers and such, but hers is a year-round Santa...all of her life. She could not tell her friends as no one would believe her. Think about it. Here is a child who has been to Santa's House, seen the frozen North Pole, fed the deer, rode in a sleigh and could do it whenever she pleased (thanks to all the props at the park).

I was always busy at Christmastime, of course. She would come see me at one of the locations I might be working at. I travel a lot and did back then too, so I was rarely home during the holiday season. I imagine her memories of childhood at Christmas are "Dad's gone again." Which I was. I can count on one hand the Christmas Eves and Christmas Days she and I have been together.

I do believe her childhood was tainted by me and my job. My wife and I told her there was a "real Santa", but I don't think the magic of Santa was ever there for her. How could it be? I did take her to see Santa when she was little, but you could see it in her eyes she wasn't buying it. After she grew up a bit, Holly often joked that if she wanted to see me all she had to do was walk into any mall and I would be sitting in center court.

Our memories of Santa relate to her and me doing things together. Each year for about eight or nine years, I would photograph her sitting in Santa's chair by herself at the park. I now have my daughter growing up in pictures in that chair. She filmed a couple commercials with me along with some print work.

I was asked by some other Santas why I just didn't try to hide the fact I was Santa from Santa's Village. That way she could enjoy the magic. How would she feel though when she found out? The daughter of a very famous Santa once told me to never hide the facts of what I do from her. In the long run, that was the best advice I ever got.

Today, I think Holly has some very fond memories of Santa and the experiences she got to have. She has a unique perspective on the whole issue. The day she was born she was Santa's daughter and the same is true to this very day. She sees me every now and then in full regalia and when people get excited to see "Santa," she just smiles and says, *"That's just my Dad."*

Thanks, Holly for sharing and this "Santa" will always keep your name in his good book.

# GIVING BACK

## By Phillip L. Wenz

Over my career I have had numerous opportunities to be involved with some great events and people. I learned early on that the "bigger" you become, the more you have to give back.

In 1995, during a hot summer's day at Santa's Village, a young boy and his parents entered Santa's House to have a visit with me. The young man looked like any other boy his age, but his parents were acting peculiar. I talked with the boy for a while, and at the conclusion, his father thanked me for my time. About two weeks passed and the same boy and his parents came back to the park. This time the boy looked different. He was losing his hair. It dawned on me that this child was sick. After talking to the child, his mother took the boy out into the park. His father approached me and thanked me. He knew of me from some publicity that was published. He told me that his son was very sick and truly believed in Santa. I thanked him for coming to the park and asked if there was anything I could do to help? *"Pray,"* he said. I took his name, phone number and then arranged for his family to have some passes to the park.

I got to know this family very well that summer, and as the park's season was coming to a close, I asked the young man what he truly wanted for Christmas. *"I want to fly with you and the reindeer,"* he replied. I was in trouble. I said, *"Let me ponder that and I'll see what I can do."* About a month passed by when I phoned his father to see how the boy was. His Dad said he was hanging in there, but all he talks about is Santa and the reindeer. I told him I was trying to think of a way to grant his wish. I had access to live reindeer, but I was sure I could not get them to fly. I told his Dad I would keep in touch.

In early November of that year, I was at a meeting of the Chicago Christmas Parade Association. During this planning session a thought occurred to me. I pulled the president of the association aside, told him of this little boy and that I had a plan. We sat in private for about an hour, and upon leaving the meeting, I knew that I could grant the boy's wish. I phoned the boy's father and told him to have his son and wife on Michigan Avenue a couple blocks north of the Art Institute on parade day.

The day of the parade I did my normal stuff, and when my call time came, I mounted the "Miracle on 34th Street" Santa float (the same float used in the re-make). I glided up Michigan Avenue into the TV zone at the Art Institute. After the TV was off, we proceeded up the street. I signaled down to the vehicle, pulling the float to stop. This was an unplanned move. No one, except the president of the association and myself, knew what was about to happen. The Jeep Cherokee, pulling the float, stopped and I signaled to one of the street marshals to come over. I told him to go over into the crowd, get the young boy, his parents, and bring them to the float. He did this with a perplexed look. As the family approached I asked the father to hand me up the boy and for the street marshal to put his parents in the vehicle. When all was in place I signaled the float to proceed with the young man standing in front of me. I handed him the reins and said, *"They are all yours. Fly'em up Michigan Avenue."*

The million plus people on the streets of Chicago saw a young boy's dream come true that day. The crowd knew something was special about this boy and cheered him. At the end of the parade route the Chicago Mounted Police surrounded the float as the boy and I disembarked. The media was in a frenzy as to what just took place. The Police ushered the boy and his family into a squad car and took them back to their vehicle. We needed to preserve this young man's identity. I got into my limo and went back to my hotel, knowing full well what was about to happen. The public relations director of the parade was instructed to give a statement. The media respected that statement and only a few photos were published of the event.

The boy died a few days before Christmas that year.

Just as in any other career or vocation, if you can help a fellow human being, you do it. I just happened to be in the right situation to "grant" his wish. It was also my responsibility.

# CHAPTER THREE

# RIDES & GAMES

# ✪ RIDES MEMORIES ✪

In August of my first year working at the park, I finally got the opportunity to realize my childhood dream of running some of the classic rides of Santa's Village. My parents made visiting the park a summertime ritual, and I spent many hours dreaming of someday working at the park and having the opportunity to drive the Fire Truck, or being the one who controlled how fast the Snowballs spun. This dream lasted with me until I was of age to get a summer job, and was the primary reason why I applied at the park in the first place. Why stand around sweating all day making fries at McDonald's when I could be operating cool machinery while working on my tan?

Being that my desire to work in the Rides Department was so strong, it was particularly cruel when shortly after getting hired I was informed that I wouldn't be able to operate anything until the age of sixteen—which wasn't happening for another three long months.

While my initial feeling upon learning this was one of great disappointment, as you'll find out in more detail later, working in the

Games Department was hands down the best job to have. This still didn't take away the sting of knowing that the perception to the majority of the other employees—especially the cute girls that tend to like older guys—was that working in Games was looked upon as the redheaded stepchild to the "cooler" Rides Department.

This disappointment lasted up until the end of the summer when I finally reached the age to drive, which in turn gave me the keys to unlock my Rides aspirations. Here is just a small sample of some of the memories that the rides of Santa's Village provided to myself and countless others.

**B**arbara Ulrich worked her first job in the Rides Department for four seasons back in the 80's. At one point she quit because she was fed up with customer service, but within two weeks of cleaning offices & homes, came back begging for her old job because she couldn't hack it in the cleaning world.

She remembers that the elephant ears always smelled damn good, and to this day, RC is still her favorite kind of soda. Besides meeting one of her best friends while training her on the antique cars, she recalls quite a few other memories from her time spent working at Santa's Village: *"Everything there was utterly surreal, from the 1950's elf heads and ornaments hanging in the storage to the little mounds of dirty diapers discarded in the park-ing lot by the visitors."*

"For the first two weeks or so of my first season, I would drop into bed totally exhausted, and then dream about operating rides. I would wake up more tired than when I'd gone to bed! The faces of the people, spin-ning by me on the rides, were distorted and creepy. Every time the ride ended, and it was time to get them off, I would wake up. This went on all night long. Eventually I became desensitized, and the dreams went away. I thought I was a nutcase until my friend confided to me that she'd been having horrible ride operator dreams! I've talked to several people who had the same dreams when they started, which made me feel a little more sane."

**She also recalls the time a kid got an unexpected shower...**
"I remember cleaning up the picnic grove during the police company picnic. My brother was in Maintenance that year. I was working near him when he was slinging the trash cans, when he pulled a particularly wet bag from a can. Just then, a little picnicker ran underneath him, as a big spray of garbage juice came spewing out of the bag—all over this little kid's head and shoulders! As he ran off crying, my brother just looked at me, raised one eyebrow, and continued along with his trash bag. I nearly peed myself laughing."

**And one particularly inappropriate song of the summer...**
"The Galleon was a new ride during my time. I liked running it because the soundtrack drowned out the nightmare-inducing music they played everywhere else throughout the park. It was catchy and upbeat. I'd spent time on it for a couple months when I finally really tried to decipher the lyrics to the perkiest song, which had a nautical sound, and was called "Pumping and Blowing." It was about a lady

who was tired of having sex and giving blowjobs! Nice selection for a
kiddie park!"

**But her favorite ride to operate was...** "The Astroliner—because I
didn't have to talk to anybody! In my last year, they just gave me that
ride every day because I preferred sitting in the 115 degree heat than to
dealing with people. I think by the end of the season, I weighed about
90 pounds, I'd lost so much water weight in that thing!"

**Speaking of rides...** "We were all afraid our rides would break
down, and hurt people. In those days maintenance was done with
duct tape and chewing gum, and some of the rides were OLD. I remember hearing one day that it was raining bolts over on the Torpedo ride!"

**But working there did have its benefits...** "I met my first ever
boyfriend there. We used to visit each other's rides during breaks and
lunches—I think he even got written up for distracting me! I dated a
couple other people from there over the years, from an Eagle Scout—to a
cokehead prep school dropout—but nothing serious, or remarkable. But
that was the best part of working at Santa's Village, meeting kids from
different schools.

**And it taught many life-long lessons...** "Not a favorite memory,
but I remember the overall contempt we workers had for the visitors.
I remember us all constantly making fun of them, but I also remember the contempt that a lot of the visitors had for us! We were hassled
about height requirements. People complained because the Christmas
Tree ornaments didn't go up and down, and countless other things. At
Santa's Village I learned a lot about dealing with people, and picked
up skills I've used in jobs throughout my adulthood."

# ARR...ME SICK OF SWEATIN' IN THE BLIMEY SUN!

**M**att Ferguson worked in Rides for three summers during the nineties, and still has all the songs from the country show that used to be performed stuck in his head. He remembers some of the good & the bad: *"It never failed that whenever the hottest day of the year was—I would be stuck on the Pirate Ship with no shade to sit in all day! The most important thing I will always have are the friendships I gained working there. It was the best summers I ever had, and I really miss Santa's Village."*

> "I used to sweat my balls off working at that place. It was like working in an oven!"
>
> - Former Santa's Village Employee

# AMTRAK APPRENTICE IN THE MAKING

**O**ne former concession worker remembers the time they got to help out: *"When the college students would leave for school in the Fall, I was asked to drive the train, which was a privilege for a Foods worker to work a ride. I drove her around the track—BACKWARDS—because I did not know how to drive stick!"*

**M**ark Bloomer spent five seasons working at The Village from 1998 until 2003. He was a Rides manager for three of those years, and worked in the Polar Dome during the off-season. It was his first job: *"I remember when I was a Rides manager, we would have parties in the office when the Rides boss was off. It was a little office upstairs in the Polar Dome. I would bring a bunch of my DJ equipment and we would party it up. Smoke machine, lights, music. It was a blast!"*

**When asked which rides he liked operating...** *"The train was fun. Turn the air pressure up on the horn. Make people go deaf. It was awesome!"*

**Ever see anything out of the ordinary?** *"I was giving this girl a lunch break on the Typhoon. She asked to ride it, and I said it was cool. So in order to ride, she's gotta take off her Rides shirt. Underneath she was wearing this halter top. She rides and it's all good. Well when she exits, she walks across the platform towards me—and her top falls down to her knees! It was great. She was so embarrassed. Wish she had bigger boobs..."*

**Ever drink on the job?** *"Some dude would give me beers in a souvenir cup!"*

**How did you deal with employees that would get out of line?** *"If you pissed me off you went on the Red Baron. No shade, gravel—sun just beat down on you and burnt you to a crisp!"*

# The Fire Truck

## By Christopher Dearman

**A**s a child, I don't think a summer went by without visiting Santa's Village at least once. Many hours were spent sliding down the Tree Slide, spinning in the Snowball ride, and spending my parents' money playing an assortment of games. While all these things were fun, by far the most exciting thing I remember experiencing was riding the famous Fire Truck ride. Sitting on the back of a real fire truck in hundred degree weather with a rubber hose to shoot water at a house engulfed in flames was pure joy. I would have ridden on the truck all day, if my parents had let me. Once I got a job working at the park, one of my goals was definitely to drive the thing.

Being that I was only fifteen when I started working that May, I knew my opportunity to steer the red truck would have to wait at least a few months until I got my driver's license. Day after day I patiently worked in the Games Department, watching the Rides manager come into the daily morning meetings to ask for volunteers to help out, yearning for the day I would have my chance. Once mid-August came and I finally got the cherished laminate that said I was legal to drive, I knew it would only be a matter of time before my dream would come true.

I still remember the fateful day that my opportunity came. One of the white shirt* Ride managers came around one morning,

---

\* WHITE SHIRT - Santa's Village employees often referred to each other by the color of the department uniforms. While this may not have always been the case, the majority of the time the colors were: white for Management, blue for Rides, red for Games, orange for Grounds, pink for Shops, black for Concessions, and yellow for Barns.

desperately asking for volunteers. I jumped at the chance to get away from the grind of trying to get people to play a game all day. I had been asked to help out in Rides a couple other times earlier in the week, but always got stuck with the shitty rides. This morning though, I guess a ton of the Ride-Os* called in sick, so he actually asked which ride I *preferred* to operate. There was no other choice in my eyes—let me get behind the wheel of the big red metal beast! To say that I was ecstatic when he granted me that wish would be an understatement. I was finally getting the good fortune to live out one of my childhood dreams.

With nervous excitement I walked over to the Fire Truck ride track. I had only gotten my driver's license a week earlier, and the largest thing I had ever driven was the neon green VW convertible bug that I had bought with money I saved up all summer to buy my first car. Graduating up to operating a vehicle that weighed many more tons was going to be quite a different experience. Little did I know what I was in for…

After arriving at the track, I found an older blue shirt Rides worker standing around waiting for the park to open. I told him that I was going to be helping out for the day, and he begrudgingly started to show me the ins and outs of working the classic ride. One of the first things I learned was that the house that was on fire didn't need water to put it out, as it actually got extinguished on its own after about thirty seconds. This was very disheartening to me, as I took putting out that fire very seriously as a child. While other kids were busy soaking everyone around me, I would be intently aiming the stream of water directly at the little house, and often was convinced that I was the one who proudly snuffed it out. Only then would I join in with the soaking of others as a form of celebration.

---

\*    RIDE-O - Slang term for a Rides worker. Similar to Game-O, Shop-O, etc.

The second thing I learned about the ride, and one alarmingly so, was that the fire truck didn't have any brakes! Let me repeat and clarify this. The ride that people were entrusting to pull them and their families around a winding track with no seatbelts, was about to be driven by a barely legal driver in a vehicle that had no brakes! Now, many people that I have talked to feel that this was just a wild rumor or urban legend*, but I can tell you for a *fact* that at least one of the four fire trucks that were used over the years did *not* have a working brake pedal. I know this because I had to drive it, and as a sixteen-year-old that just got his license less than a week before, I was scared shitless when I found out!

Inevitably, when the older operator informed me of this, my trepidation rose tenfold. *"How are you supposed to stop the damn thing?"*—was my obvious first question. He told me that it wasn't really a big deal. The truck was rigged to only reach a certain speed, so even if you floored the thing it could only reach thirty or so miles per hour. It wasn't like you could race it out on Route 90 or break any speed records.

In the back of my mind I wondered how it was possible that something like this could be allowed to operate. Weren't there government agencies that regulated the safety of amusement parks or something? Was it really going to be OK to have this huge vehicle be driven by a sixteen-year-old without the ability of having brakes to stop it? My reservations of safety and well-being were short-lived though, as it was quickly replaced with the anxiety of knowing that it was only going to be a matter of minutes before it was going to be my turn to get behind the wheel.

I distinctly remember my apprehension of climbing up into the

---

\* URBAN LEGEND - A story of unclear beginnings with little or no supporting evidence that is passed and embellished over the years. Being that Santa's Village was open over 40 years, it has many.

big rig as the experienced operator training me went through the rules of driving it. He told me that in order to actually stop the moving truck, you would have to lift your foot off the gas pedal at precisely the right time once you reached certain pole markers. Once you lifted your foot from the pedal, the truck would then slowly glide to a stop in front of the burning house or at the final exit area. When I asked him what would happen if a kid happened to fall off the thing while it was moving, he told me that there wasn't a chance in hell of the truck stopping before making road-kill, so it was the job of the guy working the microphone in the back of the truck to make sure everyone kept in their seats so that didn't happen.

When it was my turn to actually get the truck moving, I said a quick prayer to myself, and gently pushed down on the gas pedal. I quickly found out that you really had to hit the gas to get the huge truck moving, so when the older operator told me to stop being a baby and floor it, I did what he said. The truck lurched forward, and the power of controlling such a huge piece of machinery was exhilarating! After a few times around the track my nervousness went away, and I soon got the hang of it all. I was able to time the stops perfectly, and being as I had never driven anything like this before, I quickly wanted to see how far I could take it. While the gas pedal was rigged to only go so fast, if you played the curves correctly you could really get the thing moving. I spent the rest of the time before the park opened, maneuvering the thing like I was a driver in the Indy 500.

Shortly after the gates opened, the line queue quickly filled up with parents and kids eagerly awaiting the opportunity to extinguish the simulated out of control fire. As fun as it was to drive the big rig, once you actually had to take things seriously when it was filled with people, I realized that sitting in the truck's cabin all alone made for a real long and boring day. After getting back from my first break, I told the other guy that I wanted to ride in back and man the microphone for awhile. He reluctantly agreed. I quickly found out his apprehension about giving up that position when I looked back at all the hot mothers wearing bikini tops, bending over their kids, egging them on to fight the raging fire. Even better was when you would have a pretty woman wearing a white t-shirt. A quick whisper into a hyper-looking kid's ear was all it took to get quite an eyeful when he drenched the t-shirt with water. Needless to say it made things much more enjoyable for me for the remainder of the ride.

**W**hen asked if he heard of the fire truck with no brakes, a former Racing Rapids employee had this to say: *"I never saw that thing, but I heard of the stories of the "death trap" that was the Fire Truck ride. Even though I never got to see it, I definitely know of it. It's all hearsay, but if it was true—that's the funniest shit I've ever heard!"*

**A**nother employee recalls the day he learned the truth about the infamous Fire Truck ride: *"I always thought people said the thing had no brakes just to scare people, but that was no damn Urban Legend. The thing really did have no brakes!"*

# DRINKING & DRIVING & OPERATING—OH, MY!

**B**arbara Ulrich has an interesting recollection: *"I do remember that most of the time the driver on the Fire Truck was drunk. It never mattered who the driver was!"*

Various other employees seem to recall similar instances...

* "I knew some of the Ride-Os would operate some of the higher-end rides under the influence. Drunk, hung-over, puking while they're doing it!"

* "I remember some guys driving the Fire Truck and crashing it in the trees and stuff because they were hung over!"

* "That wouldn't surprise me—they had a bunch of sixteen-year-old kids operating a bunch of heavy machinery!"

* "I knew guys that would hide coolers in the forest, and refill their water bottles with beer when operating their Rides. It was 100 degree weather outside—so I didn't blame them!"

* "Those Ride-Os were pretty crazy!"

# The Ferris Wheel

## By Christopher Dearman

**B**y far the worst ride I got to operate in my short time helping out the Rides Department had to be that ancient old ass Ferris Wheel. I still have nightmares to this day about the first time I had to work it. Give me the fire truck with no brakes, or having to dodge throw-up from the riders on the Tarantula any day. Having to control that dreaded Ferris Wheel still puts a shiver down my spine, just thinking about it.

The Ferris Wheel was my introduction to working in the Rides Department, and what a horrible way to break my ride operator cherry it was. I had heard many times how people dreaded having to work it, so after I was sixteen and able to operate a ride, I was none too happy when I found out it would be the petrifying, prehistoric piece of junk they called a Ferris Wheel.

The day began with me beaming full of excitement for finally having the opportunity to work in the Rides Department. I had been waiting months for this, and even when I learned I was assigned the Ferris Wheel, I confidently walked over to Coney Island determined to enjoy myself. There was a little trepidation after hearing more than a few snickers when the manger said I would be working it, making it feel like some sort of an initiation process, but I kept telling myself all I had to do was simply push a button and pull a lever—how hard could it possibly be?

Once I arrived at the Ferris Wheel, one of the Ride Leads* was there waiting to teach me how to operate it. He told me the most

---

\*    LEADS - This was a term for the various assistant managers of the park. Usually they were not that much older then the rest of the workers, but had seniority due to working at the park for multiple seasons. One of the perks was having a walkie-talkie.

important thing was to counterbalance the people when loading and unloading the carts that the people sat in. That it was crucial to do this as the old wooden wheel had seen better days, and could not handle uneven weight. This seemed easy enough. I figured it doesn't take a rocket scientist to keep everything as equal as possible—what was the big deal? He went on to show me how the gear lever that made the wheel turn worked. Move the gear shift forward, and it moved the wheel clockwise. Pull back on it, and it slowed the wheel down to a stop. There wasn't much to it, so I figured it would be a piece of cake. Turns out I had no idea how damn scary this was going to be...

Slowly people started to trickle over to the ride once the park opened, and I quickly learned it wasn't as easy as I anticipated to balance out the wheel so that it would run smoothly. When kids were riding it was easy enough, but as soon as you had multiple adults—things got *much* more difficult. The more weight on the carts, the harder it was to force the gear forward far enough to basically lift the heavy carts up and over the top of the wheel. Get too many adults stopped between the nine and twelve o'clock position, and the weight would actually cause the wheel to start moving the wrong way in the opposite direction!

Needless to say I was now terrified of this spinning deathtrap. I kept trying to project my thoughts telepathically to everyone that came my way. *Please don't come ride this. Wouldn't you rather ride the Tarantula?* —but the people would not stop coming. This continued for the next couple of hours, and by this time I was a nervous wreck from constantly trying to keep things in order.

At this point I didn't think things could get any worse, but while looking around desperately for a break person to come save me from this wretched hell, a horrifying sight came walking toward me. My eyes grew wide, and fear crept across my body as I prayed they would just walk past me. *Nothing to see here; move along*—but alas, my Jedi mind trick did not come true. There, coming right at me, was a lady that had to weigh at least three fifty—maybe four hundred pounds—holding a huge stick of pink cotton candy in one hand, and a plastic dish of cheesy nachos in the other. Even with her relatively small child walking beside her, I knew this was going to be trouble.

Being that my break was in five minutes I figured I could stall, or at least divert her attention until my replacement came. *"Ma'am, there is no eating on the Ferris Wheel, but just down the way there is the picnic area where you can sit down, get out of the sun and enjoy your concessions!"*—I said enthusiastically, hoping I would hear a loud beeping sound like from a dump truck in reverse while she backed that huge mass of an ass out of line. I would have no such luck. She replied that she would be done by the time it was her turn to board, and immediately inhaled both concessions like a vacuum. Licking the cheese dish of the nachos so thoroughly clean that it could have been reused and resold.

Knowing I had no option but to let her on, I watched as Large Marge tried to squeeze into the small seats of the cart. Her child almost disappeared in the folds of her stomach, and I was left wondering how the kid could possibly breathe. With my hands shaking at the impending predicament that was sure to come, I pulled the restraint bar down over her triple D breasts, and watched as it comes to rest on her ample stomach—there was no turning back now.

I said a quick prayer to myself, hoping to God that the wooden wheel would hold up, and forcefully pushed the gear ahead. The cart lurched forward and I watched a huge shadow overtake me as she rose up into the air. Aware I had to time this out very carefully, I leaned on the gear until she reached the top, then pulled back on the lever to bring it to a screeching halt. Now I just needed to find enough weight to even things out.

As I looked up to see fatty licking her chops, trying to get the last of the nacho cheese from her lips, I turned my attention over to the line of people to try and find the greatest amount of heft to actually be able to counter balance her. Looking the line over I was thinking there must be some sort of Ethiopian convention in town, as the line was filled with only skinny-ass adults and malnourished-looking little children. This could definitely be a problem.

Searching all over for my damn replacement that was probably hiding out in the trees, watching me sweat my ass off from the immense stress this comical (if it wasn't happening to me) situation brought, I realized I was on my own to deal with this impending doom. Not having much choice in the matter I loaded what amounted to maybe a total of 150 pounds worth of people into the bottom cart, as a feeling of dread blasted into the pit of my stomach. With eyes closed I pushed the gear forward, hoping for a miracle. This unfortunately was not to be the case…

Looking up into the sky I saw gravity starting to do its thing. The wheel began to make a sickening noise as it lurched in the wrong direction. Scared out of my mind I pulled back on the gear to make it stop, and desperately tried to regroup. *What the hell am I going to do now?* The people in line started to realize what is happening as I tried to play it off that I know what I was doing. *Where the hell was my damn replacement?* Looking around for help that was obviously not coming, my mind started visualizing what was going to happen when I pushed the lever again. I was going to have to watch the wheel continue to turn in the wrong direction, break free of its axle, and start rolling down the walkway with terrified people screaming in terror!

Realizing I had no other option at this juncture, I slammed the gear forward again. The wheel started to moan like an elderly man trying to pass a kidney stone, and actual smoke began to spew from the apparatus. With no turning back I desperately strained to press the gear as far forward as possible, and somehow the wheel finally gave itself enough power to recover and go in the intended direction.

A sense of relief poured from my body as I immediately brought the whale of a woman to the bottom platform, and let her off. Oblivious to my now sweat-soaked trembling body, she started complaining that she only got to go around once. I'm about to make up something to the effect that it was time for the wheel's scheduled maintenance when I saw my replacement finally walking my way with a wicked smile on his face, obviously having watched this whole terrifying ordeal play out. Not about to let this slide, I tell fatty to sit tight and gladly hand off my position. Let that ass have to deal with her, as I was off to go tell Management that I had suddenly come down with a bad case of the stomach flu!

**A** former Rides employee also remembers his time working the Ferris Wheel: *"If you got some fat people up on the thing, the wheel would actually spin the opposite direction when they got to the top—the thing would start smoking! I don't even know how they got away with any of that—the place was a damn death trap! There was just no minute-by-minute supervision out there—of any kind—you would just go out there — working the Tarantula or something — and you just pressed a button—nobody maintained that! They may not want you writing about how the place was unsafe—well it was! To this day I won't go on roller coasters because of the rides there!"*

**M**ike Reeves, a former employee who worked half of one summer in the Rides Department back in the early nineties still has nightmares about having to listen to Warrant's *Cherry Pie* over & over while working the Tilt-O-Whirl. He also recalls the time he got stuck working the park's most dreaded ride: *"I remember working the Ferris Wheel—and how unbelievably unsafe the whole thing was! So there was this large couple that got on once, husband and wife or whatever, and she just started screaming the minute it started moving! Now, I don't know if she was afraid of heights or what, but I was like sixteen years old, so I'm like—yeah right, like I'm going to stop you—and besides that, you had to go all the way around at least once to get off anyway."*

*"So she's screaming, and I continue to take my time letting people off in order like I'm supposed to—but she's just up there howling! So finally, she gets back down to the platform, and I don't know if you remember that platform, but you had to step on this big lever to lift the platform up, so people had something to step off – stopping the thing from swinging back and forth".*

*"Well – she is still screaming bloody murder as they both step off that thing – and they were both HUGE – so they in turn launch me up into the air – right off the lever! So of course, because you're on the lever while at the same time holding the brake—if you get jostled off that thing—you let go of the brake!"*

*"She basically throws me off, I let go of the brake, and at the same time she vomits all over the platform! During this time, the cart they got off of swings back into them – knocking them both face first into the puke!"*

*"I lock up the brake, and they're just laying in there—and I'm like—I'm going to get help—I'm out—lets leave this to the people that are more experienced then me! The whole memory was just so horrific—you don't forget that one!"*

# LOVE THE SMELL OF VOBAN IN THE MORNING

**S**peaking of puke, one of the memories of many former workers was that of the immense amount of puking that occurred on a daily basis by the customers. It was an inevitable fact that kids, as well as many adults, would leave their lunch on the pavement for the unfortunate Grounds workers to clean up.

* "Working in Grounds I witnessed a lot of people get sick from rides, and I had to use Voban to clean up the puke—a lot."

* "The Tea Cups were notorious for causing the most protein spills!"

* "The Duck Pond was across from the Snowballs and all day long kids were throwing up at my feet! The cute Maintenance guys would come with their spray bottles with the pink stuff in it that smelled worse than the vomit!"

* "I just remember the vast amount of puke I had to mop up, working the Snowball ride—the smell was horrendous!"

* "It was one of my main forms of entertainment at that joint, making the people puke. It gave me great satisfaction to get someone to ralph who minutes earlier was annoying me—which happened quite often."

* "I always thought I had the Voban record—I had a five-bagger once. My sister, who operated rides, trained me on the Snowballs. She taught me to watch the faces of the riders, and cut the ride short when anybody looked sick. It was always a source of particular satisfaction whenever someone threw up just outside the exit gate, because then I knew I had timed it well!"

* "Learned a trick when operating the Wipe Out. You could make it spin full speed on its axis. Called it the 'Brain Scrambler'—guaranteed vomit every time!"

* "You could always tell what concession stands the kids had visited earlier in the day by seeing their stomach contents spilled all over the pavement after getting off the Snowball ride."

* "Man, I feel bad about it now but I literally made dozens of people puke their brains out while operating the Tarantula ride—most usually deserved it, but other times I just did it to break up the monotony."

* "My sister still is pissed at me to this day for making her puke from spinning the Tea Cups."

* "Once on those spinning balloons, I had a chain reaction of pukers—ten in all!"

**M**ark Bloomer recalls a time when it wasn't the customers that were puking: *"I was sick one day and no one took it seriously. I was operating the Yo-Yo and it was 99 degrees. Busy as hell. After twenty minutes of trying to load people and keep in my vomit— it unleashed right in front of everyone! Projectile vomit like I've never seen, and it was me—the ride operator. Had to sit there and clean it up. I felt like an idiot."*

# The Skyliner
## By Christopher Dearman

**A**nother thing that surprisingly brought stress to some of my days was when I had to work the Skyliner, also known as the "Sky Ride." While the loading of adults on the continuous moving seats was often comical, when it came to children trying to get on, there were times of much anxiety. I would often have nightmares of children getting rocked in the head by the moving seat, or falling between the lone skinny metal bar that was supposed to keep them in. Because of this, I would always be on edge while operating it. That said, as long as I didn't let the stress get to me, it was often fun to work on a ride that I had spent many hours on as a kid, watching my spit fall from the dizzying heights.

Most of the comedy came from the adults that couldn't comprehend how to get on a seat that continually moved. I would tell them to go stand in the yellow box, and when the seat came up behind them, just sit normal and pull down your lap bar. It really was quite simple to do, but to some this was often not the case.

Without fail there would easily be at least a half dozen people each shift that would manage to screw up the pretty straightforward undertaking. You would see people just freeze up like a deer in headlights, life flashing before their eyes. The thought of trying to sit down on the moving metal seat that was bearing down on them was petrifying. Many got tripped up and knocked down on their ass from thinking that they might get decapitated.

In actuality, the thing was moving maybe five miles an hour, but to some standing in the box waiting scared, you could tell they thought it was moving much faster. Many times the nervousness got to them and they would judge the timing wrong. The funniest moment would have to be the time where a young mother was attempting to board the ride with her two kids. For some reason she choked from the stress while trying to put her smaller kid down on the seat, and ended up pulling the kid back into her arms. This in turn sent her slightly older kid off on the ride all by himself! Being you couldn't put the ride in reverse, and also that I was just too busy laughing to stop the ride in time, she had to watch in horror as her kid ventured into the sky alone for what I'm sure was a ride the young child would never forget.

While you would think that my days of spitting off the Sky Ride to try to hit people from far above would have stopped once I reached adolescence, the thrill of watching a loogie hacked from above, falling down and hitting unexpected customers below, never got old. I know most of you will find that disgusting, but at least it was better then getting hit with another kind of bodily fluid that came from the many infamous Sky Ride hand jobs that were "rumored" to have taken place!

**P**hil Wenz also had a stressful encounter in regards to the Skyliner Ride: *"I used to sometimes walk the park as Santa, riding the rides like the Sky Ride and whatnot, but I quickly realized one day that I really shouldn't be doing that. Kids would see Santa up there, and one time we were 200 feet up when a kid pulled the lap bar up! He was like: "I'm going to see Santa!" The father quickly pulled it back down, but I never went up there again.*

# The Tarantula
## BY CHRISTOPHER DEARMAN

**M**y favorite ride to work would have to be the Tarantula ride—for a variety of reasons. During the years I worked, the ride was one of the newer, more modern rides, so you didn't have any of the stress you got when working the Ferris Wheel. All you had to do was load the ride, make sure everyone was strapped in, and push a button—it was ridiculously simple. The thing would twirl around, do its thing, and it would give you a chance to chill out for a few minutes – giving you time to flirt with a girl, or maybe sneak a quick cigarette.

If you felt like actually working and wanted to give the riders more of a thrill, there was a lever on the operating station that you'd maneuver to raise and lower the riders' carts up and down. This lever was to be used sparingly while under control so that the customers got a smooth and gentle ride. If you were in the mood for a little entertainment though, or intent on creating some mischief, this tool was the means of how you would go about it.

Let's say some punk kid was smarting off in line, making a ruckus, or acting the fool. You're most likely already hung-over from the night before, and the last thing you need is some brat making your head pound even more. So you let everyone on, making sure the kid in question sits in an outside seat. You push the button to power the thing up and let the ride get going to full speed. Once it got to optimum velocity it was simply a matter of timing the cart to let it reach the highest point, then quickly jerking the lever to make the cart plunge the dozen or so feet towards the ground. You bring him back up, and drop him again—over and over—the kid has no chance.

It usually only took four or five drops before attaining the desired effect. Sometimes you would make out the groans of the kid giving a warning, but most of the time you would just hear the splat of throw up hitting the ground. You'd look up to see the kid's head hanging over the side and puke falling from the sky!

Now it was Santa Village's policy, and pretty much just common decency that once puke was spotted, you were to immediately stop the ride and let the sick kid off. For normal everyday kids this would be strictly followed, but if you were one that was acting like a jackass in line – you'd probably have second thoughts before smarting off again once I let the ride go around a few extra times for good measure.

Another fun thing about the Tarantula was when large-breasted women would come to enjoy a spin. Using the same technique that made the brats throw up, I would let the double Ds get to the top, and slam the lever down to watch the fun bags bounce. Having too much fun, and not wanting them to throw up, I would let it spin a time or two so they could catch their breath before doing it again. Often I would get a knowing smirk from some of the appreciative dads in line.

My crowning achievement came the time that this larger woman wanted to get on the ride. She had to weigh easily over 300 pounds, and had at least triple F breasts—the things were ridiculously huge. Now these breasts were screaming to get out of her poor low-cut, stretched out top, and I made it my job to try. After a few minutes of trying to find a way to get her strapped down in the cart by having her maneuver the seatbelt between the rolls of flab, I get her locked down just as my lunch break replacement arrives. Pointing out the sloppy titties to him, I tell him to let me operate the ride one more time before I go, and to just stand back and enjoy the show.

Letting the ride spin around at full acceleration, I intently watched for the perfect moment. When her cart reached the pinnacle of height and speed, I slammed the gear down, and marveled as the hefty bags slammed into her face, smacking her hat off her head, almost knocking her unconscious! It was truly one of the funniest things I've ever seen.

# MUSIC TO THE EARS...QUEASY TO THE STOMACH

**G**eorge Strissel recalls time spent working in Rides: *"I enjoyed working the few different rides where there were two of us assigned...which always made for a good time. I can still hear the Beach Boys on the bumper cars, and the miscellaneous artists thrown together for the Himalaya. I also on occasion would pick a victim on the Spider ride to make sick...always a nice way to work in an extra paid break."*

# THAT HAD TO LEAVE A MARK

**A** former Games employee remembers regretting his choice to lend the Ride Department a hand: *"They would ask us to volunteer, and that was probably the worst thing that I could have ever done. I was making a ton of extra money on the side, working Games. When you worked a ride you didn't get shit, but a headache. One time I had to operate The Fans—these bullet-type things with fans on the back of them. They would go around in a circle and you had to stop them by hand. You would have all these stupid little kids that would try to jump out of them—it was brutal! After spending half the day dealing with this, I finally asked myself—why am I the guy that had to put myself in front of this 400 pound thing coming at me? Then there was this stupid black kid that doesn't know what the fuck is going on, and he jumps out of it. I tried to stop him and the damn thing hits me in the hammy! I get knocked over, and everyone is freak'n out about poor little Tyrone while I'm sprawled out on the ground in agony! That* *pissed me off so much that I never, ever, volunteered my services to the Ride Department again."*

# WHAT, NOT THE BURRO RIDE?

**P**hil Wenz shares his thoughts on what people remember **most often:** *"People always remember the Fire Truck ride, the Snowball ride, maybe the Christmas Tree ride—those are the rides that are always brought up the most. People could care less about the Tilt-O-Whirl and that type of stuff."*

# ✪ GAMES MEMORIES ✪

"It would be a long list to name the individuals who may have skimmed a little money while working in Games...an easier question to answer would be— was there anybody that didn't?"

"And really, when it broke down— we were all carnies— so it made sense!"

- Anonymous Former Games Employees

I t would be remiss to write about the Games Department without mentioning stealing, and the above quotes spoken by two former Games employees give this widespread dubious activity an eye-opening perspective. Yes, there was stealing going on by workers at Santa's Village...probably more so than any place I've ever witnessed. While I imagine there were many different reasons for this, being overworked and underpaid most likely was the biggest culprit. Being a cash business, the temptation to take a cut for yourself when you were sweating your ass off in the hot sun for minimum wage was enormous. The fact that you quickly learned that pretty much everyone around you was doing it, from the employees to some of the management themselves, made one's morals take a vacation during those summers for many.

*"Well if you're taking a cut — you're going to promote the hell out of your game!"*

*- Former Games Employee*

Thinking back on it now, it does give me pause knowing just how much money some of us ended up taking from the joint, but at the same time in doing so, we probably made the park a hell of a lot more money in the long run. Think about it. Are a bunch of fifteen- and sixteen-year-old kids really going to put a ton of effort into getting people to play their game? You were getting paid minimum wage to man a game whether anyone played it or not. What incentive was there to go out of your way to try and convince a bunch of strangers to pony up a buck in an attempt to win a crummy prize at a game that was almost impossible to win? By taking a cut for ourselves we in turn were making our own incentive to go out and pimp our game like no tomorrow. The more customers you had handing over dollars, the greater the opportunity you had to skim for yourself.

While morally what we were doing was wrong, and it's definitely not something I'm proud of, I know for a fact that at the end of the day I made the park a ton more money on the days I was skimming, than those I was just working for a paycheck. Even after subtracting my cut. I used to have my games packed with people. There wouldn't be a customer that would walk by that I wouldn't hit up. Whether it be acting a fool to get little kids to notice, cracking jokes and flirting with mothers and daughters to get their attention, or egging on men by calling them out on their lack of manhood—when I was taking a cut for myself, I was ruthless in my quest to get people to play.

While I don't have any accounting records to back up this statement, I would be willing to bet that the two seasons I worked in Games, the department had to be at the top of highest grossing summers in the park's history. It seemed like everyone I worked with was in on the action, and they were all like me in their vocal attempts to pimp their game for mutual benefit. Being that practically the whole Games crew was out there trying to outdo one another to make sure our games were consistently staying busy, the park was raking in the money hand over fist, and it was all done in order to make our own stealing less noticeable. The managers loved how much money you were making them, and in turn you ended up loving how much money you made for yourself.

It's funny to think back on it now, but it really was no secret that all this was going on—because virtually everyone was doing it! It was almost like we were our own Ocean's Eleven crew (but with considerably more than eleven members), and together we all helped each other make the most loot possible. We would actually have our own private pilfering meetings after the official morning

Games meetings. Once the official meetings were over, everyone that was in on the action would then gather in a group for the fifteen minutes or so before we had to go off to our assigned games. We would sit around and discuss various techniques to steal, relay any rumors we heard about Management having us under watch, and even make up contests between ourselves to see who could garner the most money that day.

My parents aren't going to be too proud when reading about all this, but they can at least take solace in knowing I wasn't the Games employee who stole enough one summer to buy a brand new Chevy Beretta! That impressive feat was accomplished by a kid who started working at Santa's Village the season before me, and his feat became the stuff of legend. Pretty much ask anyone who worked at the park during those years about the commonplace of the Games Department stealing, and usually without fail they will recall hearing about the kid who stole enough for the new car. I won't name him to protect the guilty, but I can very well attest that he did indeed exist, and that the purchase indeed happened. He actually was the one who taught me how to steal in the first place.

I still remember the day I was let in on the park's dirty little secret. Making minimum wage at the time, I rarely had money to purchase snacks or lunches. My mom would make me a bag lunch every day, and if I wanted something other than the Wonder Bread sandwich it contained, I had to use my own money to get it. Being that you couldn't walk anywhere in the park without smelling the enticing smells of elephant ears, cotton candy, and nachos, the stomach growled often for something other than what was in my brown bags. It was on one of these days a few weeks after I started working when I had the yearning to eat one of those tasty pizza puffs sold at the concession stand, yet had no money to my name. Not wanting to eat a boring sandwich yet again, I went on a search to find someone to loan me the money to get my pizza puff prize.

Being new to the park, I wasn't very close to anyone yet, so I walked through Games Alley in search of someone I wouldn't be too embarrassed to borrow money from. I didn't find anyone I was comfortable asking, and I had almost given up the hope of eating that delicious fried pizza pocket when I saw a kid working the Duck Pond who I had befriended while picking up trash in the picnic grove weeks before. Knowing I was getting paid that week, I went up to him and asked to borrow a few bucks until payday. He said no problem, reached into his pocket, and handed me three dollars. Excited that I would now be able to get my pizza puff fix, I told him I'd be sure to get him back on Friday. I still remember his casual reply: *"Don't worry about it."*

Shocked at the generosity of this kid I barely knew, I asked him why he wouldn't want to be paid back. This was twenty years ago and, while not a ton of money, it wasn't like borrowing a quarter for an arcade game—three dollars was at least enough to get you a pack of smokes. He replied that it wasn't his money anyway, it was the park's, and with that he reached into the game money belt wrapped around his waist, took out a twenty, and nonchalantly slipped it into one of his blue polyester shorts pockets.

Looking around all bug-eyed to see if anyone just witnessed this blatant act of thievery, I asked him how often he did this. I was floored when he confided that he'd get between fifty and a hundred dollars this way—every single day. He said there was nothing to it, and that everyone was doing it. Needless to say, this got my attention, and while going off to purchase my prized pizza puff, I made plans to definitely learn more about this apparent path everyone was taking to easy street.

It wasn't too long thereafter that I took the dive into partaking in this five-finger activity myself. That day came when I was walking through one of the gift shops on a break, which I did often to kill time and find new pink shirt employees to hit on. During my search I came across this adorable looking Gizmo stuffed animal from the movie Gremlins that looked exactly like the one from the movie. Being a fan at the time, and not wanting to wait for my next paycheck to purchase it, I nervously decided to go back to the Bozo Pitch game I was working and skim the $15 it cost to acquire it.

Being brought up to have good morals, I had never considered taking a cut for myself before. I mean, I literally was an altar boy at St. Mary's Church and had been raised Catholic since birth, so the commandment *Thou Shalt Not Steal* had been drilled into my head at a very early age. After hearing how everyone else was in on the action though, and especially now that there was something I greatly wanted but didn't have the means to have, I decided to take the plunge.

After getting back to my game I determined it would be best to take a dollar for every five dollars the game brought in. While I was sweating bullets with nervousness every time I palmed another dollar into my pocket, by day's end I had managed to get exactly enough money needed to purchase the Gizmo—the ease with which I attained it so quickly made me want to see how much more I could score.

In the days to come the goals I set for myself quickly grew to larger amounts. I went from taking fifteen dollars a day, to twenty, thirty, fifty, and more. Reaching the hundred dollar mark in the weeks to come was almost like winning a gold medal in the Olympics, and I soon had more disposable income than I knew what to do with. The days of eating out of brown bag lunches were gone and, along with them, my usual limitations on acquiring whatever else I desired. I had a large collection of CDs of every album I could possibly want. I owned multiple pairs of hundred dollar Oakleys, and when I became old enough to drive, my VW convertible was tricked out with a pullout Pioneer stereo, and a huge pair of speakers that took up the whole backseat. Life was good!

Since my parents had to be kept in the dark of my newfound hobby, I pretty much had to blow money on stupid stuff just so they wouldn't be any the wiser. If I was smart, I would have been putting that money into a savings account to buy something substantial, but since my parents were on my account, I would just spend it as quickly as I got it. I didn't think twice about buying cases of beer for all my friends. Saving up to buy packs of cigarettes was now replaced with buying cartons. My parents must have wondered why I was able to save money so quickly to help buy my first used car, but, since I didn't have to spend my actual paychecks on anything, I could just hand them over until I reached the amount they said was necessary. Besides, I pretty much had my very own ATM machine at my disposal at the day job to make withdrawals whenever needed.

When my first season at Santa's Village ended that summer, I had to go back to having to make do with a weekly allowance my parents generously gave me. Having to spend this on gas and other necessary adolescent needs, I yearned for the next summer to arrive so I could get back to my bountiful free money days.

When my second season finally came, the unofficial partnership I had with the park started back up like clockwork. And, despite the attempts to make things harder on us thieves, there were more people in on the action than ever. Employees in on it the season before bragged to their friends, who then got themselves hired on as well. There was a huge group of guys and girls who were regularly on the take. Despite new security measures to crack down on the pilfering, everyone had become so accustomed to the surplus of free cash; we just put our heads together to come up with ways to get around the new obstacles.

The stealing was so rampant; Management had to install lock boxes on some of the games to try to keep the money in. Instead of just collecting everything in your money belt, you now should only have the exact $100 in your belt that you started with to be used to make change. All the money actually taken in to play the game was to be put into metal boxes that were under lock and key. While this made things more difficult, it pretty much did nothing to curtail the stealing. I guess they were thinking that the customers would be the police and make sure the money was going into the lock boxes, but they never watched what we were doing. The boxes made the same sound, with or without the dollars going in it, so the system of "one for you, one for me" still held true—with the game operators just depositing a phantom dollar into the box from time to time.

After a few weeks of this, and figuring that something had to still be going on, we were informed that the customers had to now put the money directly into the boxes themselves. A rule was enacted that game operators were not allowed to touch the money at all, except when making change for larger bills. All this did was make us feel like robots rather then human beings, and make us want to stick it to the man even more.

The new procedures slowed us down some, but since the customers didn't know of this unposted rule, it really didn't make that big of a difference. As long as no one was around and the game was busy, all it would take was collecting multiple players' money all at once, and then sneaking a portion of it into your pockets. No one could tell how many dollars were going into the lock boxes, and as long as something was going in there, the customers assumed everything was legit. No one would be the wiser. If Management happened to see you handle the money, you could just feign temporary forgetfulness and say that since things were so busy it just slipped the mind. As long as the game was packed with people and money was being made, you could get off with just a warning to not let it happen again.

There were rumors all the time of our being watched, cameras being installed, spies acting like customers to try to catch us in the act, etc. While they were able to catch quite a few, I always seemed to stay two steps ahead of them. I eventually was even given a heads up from the older Leads that I was officially being watched by Management, but I was too cocky to care. I also knew they were in on the action as well so, if I went down, I figured I would just take them with me. They never would come out and admit it, but since we partied with them every weekend, after a few drinks it was hard for them to keep denying it with a straight face. It sort of became an inside joke to us all. When they kept mentioning Management was on to me, I just figured they wanted me to stop so they could get more for themselves when they went around collecting the money!

I'll get into the specifics of how my Bonnie and Clyde days ended later in the book, but for now I will say that although it was fun while it lasted, the days of being a thief ended for me a long time ago. Karma has paid me back for my embezzlement ways tenfold, and even though I haven't stole anything since my teenage years, she continues to pay me back even to this day. I've had to deal with my college dorm room robbed, my family's home robbed, and even having my identity being stolen and used in a crime spree from the East coast all the way to the West coast—so I've had more than enough stress and heartache to ever think of stealing anything ever again.

**B**esides my own stories of Games debauchery, many others were generous to share their own experiences for the book:

✳ "I worked there two summers, but eventually just moved on. The first summer you just had to work there, but the cool thing about the second summer is that you got to become the break person—which made things much easier to take a cut. Basically for the half hour you were giving someone a break, you were just ganking everything that came in! When they got back from break you handed over the money belt, alright, here you go, your game didn't make anything."

✳ "The Teenage Mutant Ninja Turtles & The Simpsons were huge during my time in Games, and definitely were not prizes at the easiest games to win. I would have to say that I may have known someone to accept payment for a very lucky winner."

* "My friend Jason got pinched for stealing at Poster Pitch–that was the one because of the eye in the sky–and they were able to look over ya."

* "I remember hearing stories about a guy that worked on one of those games where they had a microphone on–somebody–I remember hearing stories–that somebody had taken enough money from the game to buy some sort of car!"

* "Who's that one guy–Jason something? He stole enough to buy a Beretta!"

* "There was another guy there that would go around in one of those white shirts, and there was always talks of him like hiding in the woods watching people–and I'm like –don't watch me–what the hell!"

* "Man, those were the days! I get thirty or forty tax free dollars a day. Which if you did the math, made my minimum wage closer to ten bucks an hour!"

* I still have a drinking problem to this day from buying so many cases of beer on the Village's dime!"

* "I remember I was in charge of filling up the Coke machine in the break room and collecting the money. Being that they never kept inventory on how many cases of pop they had, they had no idea how much money the machine was pulling in. I would just take out the huge wad of singles each week, keep half for myself, and bring the other half to Management. It was that easy! While everyone else had to work their ass off getting people to play their game, I literally made just as much as they did in a matter of seconds—it was like hitting a slot machine jackpot every week!"

* "I used to rob that place blind!"

# Clean Your Plate

## By Christopher Dearman

While stealing was a right of passage for many who worked in Games, not all the memories of this department were so morally corrupt. I remember this one hot summer day when I was elected to work one of the new games for the season—the Quarter Pitch. In a nutshell, the idea was to try and toss a quarter onto one of three large glass plates that were attached to poles on a platform, and not have the quarter fall off. Get it to stick, and you won a huge stuffed-elephant prize.

The Quarter Pitch game looked deceptively easy, but the fact that the plate was sprayed down with a thick coat of WD-40 every morning, on top of the already slick flat surface the glass plate provided, made the odds of a quarter actually landing perfectly to stay on top practically nonexistent.

To any semi-intelligent individual, the fact that it only cost a quarter for the opportunity to win these huge, bigger-than-a-child stuffed animals should have made anyone think twice about literally throwing their hard-earned money away—but the game was quite popular nonetheless. On this particular day I worked it though, it became MUCH more popular…

Now this was in the heyday of our secret morning scam artist meetings, and while I had already figured it would be pretty simple to steal quarters from the platform with some simple sleight-of-hand, at this point in the season I had already been warned by the two older Leads that I was being watched. The Quarter Pitch wasn't located in Games Alley—it was a free-standing structure that stood completely out in the open behind the Tree Slide. Being that I didn't want to have to deal with a pocketfull of quarters, as well as having to worry about the 360 degree angles if I were indeed being watched, I decided I would take a day off from supplementing my income and just enjoy the fact that since I was far from the Games office, having to do the dreaded sales pitch of begging customers to play wouldn't be necessary. I could just count the minutes to closing while checking out the cute girls who worked at the computer printed t-shirt hut nearby. As it turned out, I would hardly have to utter any words at all to make Santa's Village Quarter Pitch history with a record-breaking money making day. Let me explain…

Shortly after pulling down the tarps that covered the Quarter Pitch platform, I set up the plates, sprayed them down, and then leaned against the fencing that surrounded the platform. There's a good chance I was hung over or quite possibly still drunk from the night before, and the last thing I wanted to do was stand around all day making change for the fools, throwing coins around.

Soon after the park opened this younger guy strolled up to me, and asked how he could win one of the giant stuffed animals for his lady. Knowing that his chances were slim to none, I barely gave it a thought as I made change for his dollar. I explained he had to get a quarter to stick on the plate, and went about my girl watching.

It couldn't have been more than ten seconds later that this guy let out a yell, and started high-fiving his girlfriend. *What the hell?* He started telling me which one of the huge prizes he wanted, and still in shock, I reluctantly went to get him his prize.

Now, the Games manager John had mentioned before that these prizes cost like eighteen dollars apiece or something, so immediately I knew my game was in the hole—and I hadn't even been open for five minutes! Since I always sorta rooted for the customer anyway, the whole sticking-it-to-the-man attitude of my youth, I didn't feel too bad about his success....until right away he threw another quarter—and wins AGAIN!

*Are you fuck'n kidding me?* The guy danced around like he just won the lottery, and I immediately jumped up on the platform to see how the hell this fool won twice in a matter of seconds. *Did he stick a piece of gum on the back of the quarter or dab on some sort of glue?* My mind was racing trying to figure out how this kid did the impossible, but when I picked the second winning quarter off the plate, it was as clean as a whistle.

I begrudgingly gave him his second choice of huge-ass prizes, but when he started to play again I got in front of him to put a stop to this obvious quarter con man. I told him that I had to invoke the unposted rule that any one person could only win two large prizes per game, per day. He got in my face, fussing and moaning that it didn't say that anywhere, but I quickly pointed out that for less than a buck he had more prizes than one person could handle. He cussed me out a bit, but after realizing I wasn't going to allow anymore of this nonsense, he and his girl left with their hands full, smiles plastered all over their faces.

Now the good thing (or in my case bad thing), was that with all the hoop'n and hollering the cat did as he won, a large crowd of people started to surround the Quarter Pitch pagoda, each wanting to get in on a piece of the action. I was making change left and right, and quarters were raining down all around me. The game was hopping, and I started to calm down a bit after realizing that the free publicity of the two large prizes being carried around the park would bring in more than enough business to cover the thirty-six dollars worth of inventory that had already been won. Turns out that this sense of calmness ended up being short-lived...

Not more then a half hour later, I heard the dreaded "ting" of a quarter landing on top of a plate yet again! This was soon followed up by another...and then another! It was like I was in some bad episode of the Twilight Zone. Every time I heard the sound of the quarter landing was like Pavlov's dog knowing what was going to happen next – my ass was going to get fired!

By this time I was quickly running out of inventory, and Management had caught wind of the fact that there was a herd of elephants being carried around the park. We all had been warned that if any of these big ticket items were won – i.e. given away or sold – that our job was on the line. I wasn't doing anything shady, but had already handed out six of them before lunch!

A little more time went by, a couple more prizes were won, and even though the game was overflowing with quarters everywhere, at this point I was already sick to my stomach. By the time two of the Game Leads came over to investigate, I was close to spewing chunks from nervousness. Having partied with both many times, they had no problem coming up to me to ask what the hell I was doing, obviously thinking I was pawning the prizes for cash. They both knew of my five-finger activities, and were positive I must have been selling the things off. I told them that everything was legit; I didn't sell *any* of them, and at this point didn't want anything to do with this damn game! They weren't buying it, and walkie-talkied John to come over.

A few minutes later he came strolling down the path with a look of—*Really Chris, you really expect me to believe that for the last month NO ONE had won a damn elephant—and you have given away eight of them before noon!* I pleaded to him that I was doing nothing wrong—I mean, I used to be an altar boy! *"I swear to God that all these people were legitimately winning!"* Luckily as he was standing there deciding what he was going to do with me, another customer tossed up a quarter that landed. *"I told you I wasn't lying!"*

Seeing was believing, but obviously something was not right with the game. He told the customers that we were closing it down for a few minutes, as he climbed up on the platform to check the plates. It turned out that one of them was not properly positioned on the pole, giving it just enough of a tilted slope to slow down the quarters enough to stick.

He started to bitch me out that I should have known something wasn't right from the start, but I wasn't going to go down for this. *"Am I supposed to be an engineer of proper plate positioning? I didn't sign on for that! They were set up when I got here. I'm just supposed to make change, not determine the aerodynamics and physics of quarter tossing!"* Disgusted, he told me to hand over my money belt, and for the rest of the day he had me working in the picnic groves picking up garbage. Was that any way to treat the guy that single-handedly brought in the most money that Quarter Pitch has ever seen?

# FUTURE GAME SHOW HOST

Speaking of "giving away" the merchandise, one former employee remembers actually doing so, but at least it was for good intentions: *"I worked there one season in the late eighties. I had worked various jobs before that, but this was the first one I wasn't flipping burgers. I never stole any money, but I did get in trouble when I was caught giving away the merchandise. I felt really bad when little children would lose, so I would just give them a prize anyway!"*

Dave Decker, who hated the dreaded blue shorts, worked in the Games Department for two summers back in 1989 and 1990. Wanting to stress to his friends, family & employers that all this happened a long time ago, and that he wouldn't dare do some of the things he did back then now, he recalls his first day: *"When I first started – I showed up with my buddy Kale, and the first thing we do is walk into the park where we were immediately*

told to go over to the Skyliner. We go over there and see the thing lying in pieces, and they end up making me in charge of helping these guys put this thing together—nuts and bolts and everything! I'm only sixteen years old putting this shit together! This is my first day, and I have no idea what the fuck I'm doing—Oh, just make sure they're tight – I'm like, yeah that's smart...it's only a 200 foot drop!"

**After finally getting to work on the actual games...** "I once was in Coney Island working a game, and I had a customer come up to me. He makes a comment about the stuffed animals I had to offer—because they were some ugly-ass prizes. He taps his side, and says: Well thank god I have this – and I look down to see that he has a gun!"

"So I go tell my bosses that this guy has a gun, and now I have to walk around with these guys on my break looking for him. I end up pointing him out, and security approaches – they find the gun, but turns out he's a cop or something. So they move me to another game, and somehow this fuck'n crazy drunk cop finds me! He comes up and is like: You're lucky I don't shoot you!—and I was like wooah dude—you had a gun in a family park - you can't be doing that!"

## Did you ever get to help out at Racing Rapids?

"Nope—but I dated a lot of chicks from there though! We would break into the place on our day off, and ride the Tilt-O-Whirl, and the pirate ship—everyone likes the pirate ship!

## Did you have a favorite Game to work?

"We used to always pick Tin Can Alley—the reason was that we would get those Racing Rapids chicks to come up and demonstrate how the games were played on their breaks. Now if you notice our line of sight

*standing up on the platform, since they were still wearing their swim-*
*suits—we get to have a cleavage shot of all the girls while they were*
*grabbing the balls and throwing them in!*

### Any other reason for picking that game?

*"Oh that, and also that we probably pocketed something like 100 bucks*
*a day on top of our pay when we worked it!"*

### So you were one of the parks many unofficial partners?

*"Who wasn't? It was one of the perks of working in Games. For those*
*who were stealing—oh, my god—couldn't have been easier. Everyone*
*wanted the good games—especially the good money-making games.*
*Getting a new pair of Oakley's every fuck'n week was very nice!"*

### What else did you spend Santa's Village's unknowingly gener-ous profit sharing on?

*"Drugs—beer—dates—not like prostitutes, but we like took chicks out—*
*gas for the car – getting the car washed. It was just the summer of fun—*
*we were financed to the gills man—we were in the gold! Remember*
*when the video game Street Fighter first came out and we were all*
*ganking money to exchange it into rolls of quarters. On our breaks we*
*had Street Fighter championships in the arcade room."*

### What's the most you ever took from a game?

*"I forgot what game it was, but it had the milk jugs—the ones where*
*you had to throw the softball in there to win. Now, this is right around*
*the time when Super Mario Brothers came out – and you know—you're*

*fuck'n sixteen years old, and when you have a guy come up to you, saying he'll give you fifty bucks for that Mario doll—I'm yelling out: We have a WINNER!"*

*"Then Management would come up to me and be like: OK, Dave— there's at least five Mario and Luigi dolls walking around when these things should be damn near impossible to win…and I'm like dude it was their lucky day - they got lucky, man!"*

*"That and the Tin Can Alley game were the biggest money makers— which was insane. Tin Can Alley had this metal bridge with a lip on it right up above the game. We would crumple up ten-dollar bills and throw them up there until we had a bunch of them lined up. Then when the shift guy came over to relieve us for breaks—we just grab it! We'd go buy our chicken sandwiches from concessions, and then it was Street Fighter time."*

## Did you end up getting fired from there?

*"I think we all did—because we were slackers."*

## So what do you think about looking back almost twenty years later?

*"It's crazy – we actually did all that? But, honestly, if you look at the jobs kids have now compared to what we had—what we actually expe- rienced and went through—we had great times working there. There was a slogan Games workers had: Overworked, underpaid, games, games, games – which was true—except for those like us that made sure we weren't!"*

# FIGHT THE POWER

**W**hile some employees got fired for their transgressions, others left on their own terms: *"I remember quitting. There was this bald manager, and he was upset that the game I was working wasn't making more money. He was standing in front of everybody, telling me what I should do, and I thought to myself—you know what, I don't need this job, I'm doing this for fun, and here's this guy barraging me in front of customers! As he walked away, I whistled at him — and of course that made him mad. I remember calling him by his first name to come over. I undid my money belt and I'm like — if you think you can do a better job than me, fine — YOU run the damn game—and I left!"*

# A TREASURE TROVE OF FUN

**O**ne former Games employee recalls the time he got punished for being late to the morning meeting, and was assigned to hose down the plastic ball pit because some kid used it as a public bathroom. *"When I arrived at the playground my nose hairs were immediately singed by the putrid smell of old urine. Fighting back the urge to puke, I blasted the balls with the hose, which only kicked up some more piss, making the smell even worse! I sprayed them down for about sixty seconds, then got the hell out of there. I could only imagine what else could be lurking underneath the rainbow-colored sea of balls."*

# IF YOU GOT TO GO, YOU GOT TO GO...

**A**lways looking for ways to cure boredom, pranksters could have fun by sneaking up behind the people at the Shooting Gallery game and take a flash picture. *"It was especially fun to creep up behind a co-worker that was in charge of making change, and set the whole place off. It would be like Armageddon with all the bells and whistles glaring loudly. I may even have made one kid piss himself!"*

**A**nother employee remembers the Shooting Gallery for another reason: *"I remember the guy in the Shooting Gallery that was playing the piano, but he really wasn't playing—just bobbing up and down—so gay."*

> "Was my first job. Worked in Games. Such ugly outfits."
>
> — Former Employee Tania Binning

# GUESS WHO?

**O**ne former Games employee had this to say when asked if he remembered a certain Games Lead: *"Yeah, I remember him. He had a big head. Walked around with his white shirt—fuck'n chaw in his mouth—radio—and you know, if I was twenty-one at that time, I would be that way, too. Who wouldn't be?"*

# BOWLING FOR DOLLARS

**R**ealizing the place was filled with gamblers, one former employee remembers learning the trick to a full stomach: *"I remember at the beginning of one summer I requested that game Roller Bowler for like a week straight - practicing over and over until I could win it every time. For the rest of the summer I would bet suckers lunch money that I could win in one try. I ate for free at least a dozen times!"*

# Scarred For Life

## BY CHRISTOPHER DEARMAN

**S**hortly after starting working at the park, I quickly became friends with a Games employee who had worked the season before. He was your typical cool kid, wannabe James Dean type, that definitely was a hit with the ladies—just the type of kid I was hoping to be. I had met him on my first day, and this being my first real job, I tried to latch on to anyone who could walk me through what to expect. Acting as a mentor figure to the ways of the park—eventually even including how to rob the park blind—he was one I took to looking up to, even though we were basically the same age.

Being fifteen and in the midst of trying to find my own identity, I had the bright idea to get my ear pierced. Mind you, this was at a time where it was actually cool to have bling in your ear, as long it was in your left one and not the right. I have no idea if this still holds true, but at the time having your right ear pierced suppos-edly signified one's affection for having a limp wrist in the days of pre-political correctness. Seeing that my new friend rocked a real diamond stud in his left ear, I confessed my desire to become part of the earring movement to him, and he enthusiastically told me to bring an earring with me to work the next day. *"Why pay fifteen dollars to have someone do it, when I'll do it for five?"* Thinking that was pretty good logic, and assuming he must own an earring gun or something I told him I would, and immediately got excited with anticipation for what tomorrow would bring.

After convincing my mom to take me to Spring Hill Mall under the guise of needing another pair of work shorts, I endured through the pain of having to try on numerous pairs of blue shorts from the clearance rack at Sears. After my mom found some that she could work with (being the only pairs that came close to fitting went past my knees and needed to be hemmed), I told her that while she checked out, I wanted to visit a few stores on my own. We made plans to meet back up in thirty minutes, and I raced out of the store. I would have just enough time to make a run to The Earring Tree store that resided in the middle of the mall to make my prized purchase.

After working up a good sweat from my speed walking, I fever-ishly reached my destination—The Earring Tree—a store that was basically filled to the brim with a shit load of different earrings. After spending some time gazing into the glass display cases, I was asked by a saleslady if I needed any help picking out a pair. Being one of champagne tastes at the time, I told the lady I was looking for diamond studs. I can only guess that she thought I was looking for a gift for my mother or girlfriend, so she took out a few pairs in various sizes. I deliberated for quite some time before picking out what I thought was the perfect pair and asked how much they cost. Flipping over the box, the lady informed me that the pair in question was three hundred dollars. *"Are you fuck'n kidding me lady?"*—I wanted my ear pierced, but not that bad. I was only fifteen, barely making minimum wage, and this bitch was trying to make a commission check from my ass!

The look on my face must have said it all. With head down I started walking away when I heard: *"Well I suppose you could get some fake Cubic Zirconia ones which are much cheaper, but I'll warn you, whoever you give them to will NOT be happy"*—she said in a snooty tone. Instantly my eyes lit up. It never occurred to me that they would even make such a thing as fake diamonds. *Why the hell didn't you tell me this before?* Telling her to let me see some of this mythical fake merchandise, I immediately came to the realization that the $9.95 ones look indistinguishable from the three hundred dollar pair. *What kind of idiot would even consider buying the more expensive ones?* I quickly paid for the diamond knock-offs, and left thinking it would be a cold day in hell if a woman ever conned me into forking over that much dough for the real things. Just another scam like Sweetest and Valentine's Day, created by women to waste more of men's money!

Leaving the store beaming, I stuffed the bag that contained the small earring box into my pocket, and hurried back to Sears to meet up with my mother. Daydreaming of going to work the next day during the drive home, I made no mention to her of my stealth purchase. I knew full well my parents would put the cabash on any plans of puncturing my body permanently, even if I just uttered my desire to do so. It would be much easier to just get it done, and then hide it from them until I turned eighteen. I mean, how hard would it be to hide a little hole for a little over two years? I would just put it on when I got to work, and take it off before I left—piece of cake.

The next morning I was up before my mom even had to wake me, which in those days was rare, as I would easily sleep past noon if she let me. Getting ready for work, I was bubbling with excitement, knowing that in just a couple hours I would become one of the "bad boys"—thinking that a fake diamond stud in my ear was the ticket to having my pick of any girl at the park.

Once I was dressed, I pulled back the corner of my waterbed where I would hide all sorts of contraband from my parents— cigarettes, lighters, pinups of naked chicks I pilfered from various Playboy magazines over the years, etc. I fished out the bag that had The Earring Tree logo on it, and stuffed the whole thing in my newly-hemmed itchy blue shorts.

The ride to the park was one of great anticipation. My mom had no idea that she was driving her only son to where he was about to scar himself for life. After arriving, I quickly punched in, and eagerly went to the Polar Dome where everyone met for the morning Games meetings. Seeing my new buddy, he immediately asked if I had the goods, and I proudly displayed my fake diamonds. Flipping the box over to see the price tag, he commented that I better not blame him if my ear turned green. This cat claimed he pulled at least a hundred dollars a day from his five-finger activities when working games, so he of course had the real deal. I told him that that shit didn't matter to me, I just wanted to get my ear pierced already. He just shrugged—*"We'll, it's your ear."*— and told me we could do it as soon as the meeting was over.

So the meeting started up and we did the usual competitions

and trivia questions to decide who gets to work what game, and somehow I ended up getting the dreaded Duck Pond. It was easy enough to work, but you had to deal with whiny kids complaining all day when they didn't get the prize they wanted—so needless to say I wasn't too happy. The other shitty thing about the Duck Pond was that it had to be up and running a half hour before any of the other games. Being that it was near the entrance, someone had to man the game as soon as the gates opened in order to squeeze every dollar out of the parents whose kids inevitably would sprint full speed to the game as soon as it was spotted.

Disappointed that I wouldn't have any time to get my ear pierced before work started, I informed my friend that I had to run the Duck Pond. He said not to worry, it would only take a few minutes, and that he would get the necessary supplies and meet me there before having to go man his own game. Brimming with excitement I went to the blue metal structure that held the water trough filled with dozens of DayGlo colored ducks, and removed the tarp covering the thing. Opening up the side to turn on the water flow that moved them, I looked in at the locker mirror that was conveniently placed to check on how your tan was coming along. Taking out the thick black plastic comb that I kept in my back pocket, I moved the hair away from my ear, trying to imagine what it would look like after I de-virginized it in just a few short minutes.

Looking over to my left across the way, I saw my friend coming towards me with a wicked smile on his face. I'll be honest—at this point I started to get second thoughts. *Was I really going to let this guy do ear surgery on me? I could just go back to The Earring Tree someday and get it done by a professional for fifteen bucks—why chance it?* Deciding that I had gone this far, and not really wanting to have to wait another day longer, I convinced myself that it was now or never.

He came up to the Duck Pond and asked if I was ready to do this. In one hand he revealed a paper towel, holding a big ice cube; in the other, a long sewing needle.

*"Wait a minute, you didn't say anything about any pin...what the fuck is going on here?"*—I shouted, starting to get worried.

*"I'm going to pierce your ear."*—he said with no hint of this being a cruel joke.

*"Well, where the hell is the earring gun?"*—I asked, fully realizing that there wasn't going to be one.

*"Only pussies use that shit. Relax, I've done this dozen of times."*

As he said this I start wondering how the fuck I got myself into this situation. Seeing my trepidation, he told me to chill out and informed me this is how he did his. My gut told me he was lying through his teeth, but I couldn't chicken out now. I mean, how bad could it be? I had heard of this technique being used before. I didn't actually know anyone who had done it this way personally, but I assumed this is how it had to be done in jail, the ghetto, and in trailer parks. *Wasn't I man enough to do it this way as well?*

Because I had already informed everyone that I was soon going to be sporting a diamond stud—I couldn't possibly back out now. He told me to hold the ice cube on my earlobe for five minutes, while he went off to go find a pen I could use to mark the exact spot I wanted the hole to go. Watching him walk away I held the ice to my ear, and quickly felt it going numb. *What the hell did I get myself into?*

A few minutes later I saw one of the Leads coming my way to give me my bank belt for the day. Immediately the thought of faking an illness and having him send me home so I wouldn't have to go through with this raced through my head. Seeing the ridiculous situation I was currently in, he asked why I was holding an ice cube to my ear. Shaking his head after telling him, he walked away laughing, and I was left standing there with ice water dripping all over my red Games shirt. I keep telling myself this will all be worth it once the chicks come flocking.

After what seemed like an eternity of waiting, my friend came back with the pen and told me to remove the ice. Asking for advice on exactly where it should go, I took the pen, and used the locker mirror to pick the spot he recommended for the puncture. He asked if I was sure, and I get the sense that he was a little shocked that I would actually go through with this. It was then that I realized—this bastard had never done this before!

Too late to turn back, I pulled my wallet from the blue shorts, stuck it in my mouth and bit down. I shut my eyes tightly, and felt him grab onto my earlobe. Bracing myself for the immense pain I knew would be coming, he said he was going to count to three. *Just do it already!*—I screamed in my head, about to pass out from anticipation. One...he said slowly...two...he said even more drawn out....THREE! He lunged the needle into my flesh, and I heard a loud "pop"—and immediately my body gushed with pheromones at the sensation of being violated. The first ridiculous thought that comes into my mind is: *This must be how it feels when a girl pops her cherry!*

To my surprise, it is over rather quickly. My ear is still frozen, so there isn't that much pain. I asked him if I could glance in the mirror. From the look on his face I could tell that he was a little queasy from what he had just done. He suggested I should probably wait until the needle was out. I took out the box, removed one of the studs, and handed it to him to finish the job. After putting the thing on me I quickly took a look in the locker mirror and lo and behold, looking back at me was a gleaming fake diamond stud. I had to admit; in my eyes it looked pretty damn cool. I thanked him for his assistance, and he reminded me of the five bucks I owed him. *Damn, I could have done this myself,* but pay the man nonetheless. He walked off five dollars richer, and I was left working the Duck Pond for the rest of the day with my new prize.

At the end of the day I ran into him again, and he asked how my ear was feeling. At this point it was starting to throb a bit, but I didn't let on to anything. Having had the pleasure of showing off my new bling to all the cuties throughout the day and all the adulation it brought me, I could deal with a little thumping in the ear. Thinking of all the possibilities of the different kinds of earrings I could now adorn myself with, I told him I couldn't wait to dangle a silver cross from it. Of course I could only wear a stud at work, but after-hours I could wear whatever I wanted—the more outrageous, the better.

The excitement of all the potential new looks I could create for myself was exhilarating. Unfortunately, this was short-lived. He took this opportunity to inform me that I would need to leave the earring in for at least a week before I changed it, or else the hole would close. *Uh...come again? Are you fuck'n kidding me? My mom is going to be here any minute to pick me up!* Trying to hide a little hole is one thing, but having this gleaming fake rock in my ear is another. I'm about to go into cardiac arrest right then and there when he tried calming me down, and told me to just go to First Aid and get a Band-Aid to cover it up. *That just might work! My mom will never know!* I went to the nurse in the front office and informed her that someone cut their finger on the Tree Slide. After she handed over the life saving Band-Aid, I went to the bathroom to cover the earring and hope for the best.

Seeing my mom pull up to the front gate in her black Monte Carlo, I slowly walked over and got in the passenger side. Figures it would have to be my left ear which was pierced, which is now directly facing her. After getting in the car she asked how my day went. Holding my hand on my ear to try and cover the bandage, she quickly realized I was trying to hide something and asked what was wrong. Desperate to change the subject I tried telling her I cut it while bumping into a tree, but mother's intuition got the best of me. She told me to remove the Band-Aid so she could take a look, and realizing the inevitable I took off the bandage. All my plans of spending the next two years hiding the thing flew out the window. At that moment, I hadn't even had it in for a full day and not only am I now scarred for life, I also have to spend the rest of the car ride wondering how the hell I'm going to explain this to my father!

# I CAN SEE! I CAN SEE!

One Games employee recalled the time he decided to fight boredom on an extremely slow day by using a wooden stick from the infamous cane races\* as a tool to act like he was blind: "I was wearing a pair of $120 black Oakleys that was acquired with money I stole from a game earlier in the week. I was tapping the ground through Games Alley haphazardly like a blind man stumbling around after a few cocktails, doing a bad Al Pacino 'Scent of a Woman' impersonation while trying to impress my fellow bored co-workers. I was knocking into walls, feeling around in the direction of any large rack that came my way, and generally making an ass out of myself."

---

\*   CANE RACES - A game used by Games management sometimes during the morning meetings to determine who got to work the popular games. Primarily done for the enjoyment of seeing people make fools of themselves, the object of the game was to put one's forehead on a cane that is touching the ground and then circle your body around it a set number of times. Once you complete the required amount of rotations you then have to attempt to run and find a prize somewhere in the Polar Dome. Inevitably you would fall on your ass - sometimes multiple times - due to the dizziness that was created.

"Things were all in good fun until I started paying more attention to this cute girl I was trying to impress with my Ray Charles antics who was working the Ring Toss, rather then seeing this small Mexican child standing right in front of me. It wasn't until the mother of the child started to scream out in horror, pulling the boy out of supposedly harm's way, that I realized my innocent antics might not be one of my smartest ideas."

"Now I don't know if the fact that I could actually see perfectly fine wasn't comprehended due to the language barrier, or that it just wasn't a good enough excuse in her opinion, but the woman got up in my face and started spewing an array of Spanish words in my direction, which I could only imagine weren't compliments. I ripped off my shades in order to try to calm the frantic lady down, trying to convey that her son was in no imminent danger and that I was only goofing off, but she stormed off in hysterics anyway. I spent the rest of the afternoon feeling terrible, and needless to say, I never did an encore of my Stevie Wonder Act again."

# LIFE'S NOT SO BAD WHEN YOU CONSIDER THE ALTERNATIVE

After getting fed up with having to pick up trash after working all day in the hot summer sun, one Games employee found a unique way to get out of garbage picking duty: "After a few weeks of having to clean the parking lot of trash every evening, I decided I had enough and volunteered to work the Duck Pond everyday - the only game that stayed open till parks close. Management thought I must be up to no good, because NO ONE wanted to work the Duck Pond, so I think I was even put under surveillance for suspicion of stealing after a few days of enlisting for the wretched job. I swear though, I was doing nothing of the sort—I just hated picking up people's *trash! There was a definite trade off though. While I did get out having to collect litter for that last hour, I found out that having to deal with screaming kids that refused to leave was torture in its own right. After a week or so of leaving with migraine headaches every night, I gave up on the experiment, and went back to walking the lots with everyone else."*

## SURE HE'S NOT THE ONLY ONE

**W**hen asked about his favorite game, John McMillion replied: *"Don't recall exactly what it was, but it always had someone on a microphone. I used to love that one because they always use to put a hot looking young girl on the mic!"*

# Jawbreaker

### By Christopher Dearman

**W**hile I've heard of many life-threatening situations that have occurred at the park over the years, this is one of the few that happened right before my very eyes. It was a dreary day, raining off and on, and most of the customers had already left the park. I was working one of the games in Games Alley, and most of the day was spent alternating between staring at my watch, and praying that the manager would hurry up and close up shop early.

Bored out of my mind, I passed the time daydreaming of all the naughty things I wanted to do with this cute little brunette girl who tantalizingly worked a few games down from me. Just when my fantasy was getting to the part where she was moaning for more, I heard something completely the opposite of pleasure. It was a gut-wrenching noise—one which I can only describe as something like a dying emu waiting for someone to pull out a gun, and put it out of its misery. Needless to say this was not anything like the sounds I expected to hear from my vivid mental imagery.

The groaning started getting violently louder, and I start searching around to see what the hell was making this sickening commotion. Finally, I located the source of this miserable sound by looking up towards the second story Games office. There I saw Shane—this lanky, tall drink of water looking kid—standing on top of the stairs, clutching his throat. He was obviously choking on something.

Never having witnessed anything like this before except on TV, I looked around desperately for somebody to do something. The rest of my fellow employees had the same shocked looks as I, as we all watched Shane's face quickly turning to a sick shade of blue. At this point I was thinking this kid had no chance.

A few more tense moments went by, and Shane's now as blue as a Smurf. His eyes bulged out like his head was being squeezed by a vise-grip, and he was seconds away from passing out cold. Just when I thought his goose was cooked, out of nowhere a white shirt Lead named Bob hurtled up the stairs in a flash. In one fluid motion he wrapped his arms around Shane's waist, turned him to face the stair railing, and performed a perfectly-executed Heimlich Maneuver—like something right out of a movie.

After the sharp thrust to his gut, a ball like object flew from Shane's mouth and sailed through the air. Seemingly in slow motion, it fell from the sky until it finally hit the black pavement below. After a few bounces, the object came to a slow roll down

Games Alley. Only then did I realize that the object that almost took Shane's life was a multicolored jumbo jawbreaker!

As Shane was hunched over the railing gasping for air, Bob raised his hands triumphantly, as the various onlookers started clapping in appreciation for the life-saving miracle they had just witnessed. After recovering a bit, Shane rightfully started thanking him over and over for saving his life, as Bob strutted down the stairs, head held high like a matador after slaying a bull.

Word spread quickly throughout the rest of the day of Bob's heroics. Young girls from all over the park came up to him gushing, and Bob milked it for all its worth. I can't confirm anything for sure, but from the looks on all the young girl's faces, I can only imagine he had his pick of the "groupies" later on that night!

**D**ave Dekker also recalls the same incident: *"I personally was never injured and never really ever witnessed any injuries, but I definitely heard about the time Shane was so happy that it was raining and the park was going to close early that he inhaled a jawbreaker and got it stuck in his throat! I heard there was a stream of blood, and he ended up needing the Heimlich! He ended up calling me afterwards to tell me of his life-and-death experience."*

**O**ther than almost being the location of Shane's demise, the Games office was one of those places where if the walls could talk, I would have more than enough stories to fill this book on its own. Located in what was basically a big attic above the arcade across from Games Alley, this tree house-like thing reeked of stale air and disorganization. You would climb these badly painted brown wooden stairs and open the door to find a couple of desks covered in a mess of files, paperwork and empty food containers. In back was a makeshift area where they kept the prize inventory from years past that weren't being held with the fresh stuff in the Polar Dome. It basically was a dump, but at least it wasn't near the owners and higher-up's offices in the front of the park, so it lent itself to much hijinx. Many former employees recall its being used for things other than day-to-day operations and storage:

* **Man, I can't tell you how many times I brought up my fellow female co-workers on a search for inventory to stock a game, and somehow convinced them to give me a blow-job while back in that attic!"**

* **"I remember I slept out one night in the stuffed animal attic after an all-night drinking Risk extravaganza!"**

* **"We used to play poker in there all the time after-hours. We would just hide in the park until after closing, and then use one of the Lead's keys to get into the office. We had beer chill'n on ice all afternoon in hidden coolers, and we would drink it all through the night while gambling. The best part was that after we passed out, we woke up already at work for the next day!"**

* **"I used to have some of the Leads buy me bottles of peach schnapps because I knew the girls loved the stuff. I'd give them cash in the morning, and later that afternoon I'd go up in the Games office and magically there would be a pint or two waiting underneath a box of old stuffed teddy bears in back!"**

> * "I remember that the Games office
> basically was a converted attic so it would
> get hot as hell up there. There was this one
> time that I got pissed off at the bald Games
> manager that hung out up there. For like a
> week straight I would sneak up there every
> day and piss in the corner—just waiting for
> the stench to drive him nuts!

# The Wacky Wire

## By Christopher Dearman

**D**uring my second season the Games manager unveiled a brand new game for the Games Alley. I
remember him being giddy as a schoolboy when he told everyone, knowing that the odds of winning the game were next to
none, yet it would draw customers in like a magnet. The "Wacky
Wire" was basically a metal rod that spun around twisted like a
corkscrew. You had to take a small wire wand with a metal hoop,
and traverse it down over the corkscrew until reaching the bottom.
This had to be done without the insides of the metal hoop touching it at any point. If the wire even breathed on the metal, a loud
embarrassing buzzer would go off, signaling you had lost the
game—along with your dignity.

Wacky Wire looked relatively easy but was deceptively hard.
The corkscrew part wasn't necessarily too difficult. If you had a
steady hand, you just had to get in to a little rhythm and slowly

work your way down. The problem came when you got to the very bottom. This is the point that would set the buzzer off without fail. I can only recall one customer actually ever winning it—and there was controversy whether the white trash punk wearing jean shorts and a wife beater t-shirt somehow cheated by sticking a pinky in the hole or something.

The trick to winning was you had to maneuver the wand over the ninety degree right angle at the bottom in the opposite direction that you had been moving the whole time. You had to speed up the wand movement to catch up to the right-angle, and quickly twist your hands to get around it. Because this was extremely difficult, the manager filled the booth with the most expensive prizes of the park. For a buck a shot people would literally drop dozens of dollars trying to win.

The beauty of the game was that the loud buzzing would draw attention and bring other customers into the mix. On busy days there were five of them going at all times, and because the average time before people would bust out was approximately five seconds, the game would rake in hundreds of dollars a day.

Of course, everyone who worked at the park wanted to learn how to win the Wacky Wire. There was a race by the employees to see who would be the first to conquer it. Breaks and lunches were spent practicing trying to achieve this badge of honor, and after a few days word got out that one of the Game-O's, we'll call him Kirk, had been the first one to attain success.

Kirk was a kid who started working that season and quickly became the quasi leader of the crew of kids I rolled with due to being older than us all. He was a crooked cat who contributed to our delinquency by buying beer, getting bud, and just adding to everyone's shady ways. After figuring out the trick to winning, he refused to let us in on the secret, and strutted around like a king.

His reluctance to sharing it burned my ego deep inside, but this could also be due to the fact that a girl I had been crushing on at the time latched onto him, spending the money he stole from the park on her like a sugar daddy.

With the added incentive of wanting to knock this guy from his pedestal, I used my second-season seniority to volunteer working the booth as many days as it took to become a Wacky Wire wizard. I practiced every minute I could, and after a day or two I finally figured out the trick to winning. I still remember my first successful attempt—the sense of accomplishment was incredible. As soon as I knew the solution everything just sort of clicked, and I could win at will. I became a Wacky Wire guru. Not only could I get it to the bottom each and every time, eventually I would even win races with the other employees who could accomplish the feat—even Kirk.

Having the expertise of the Wacky Wire game in many Games employee's arsenal, there were many stories of our putting the skill to good use. Like the times we went to the Kane County Fair—the yearly summer carnival in which my crew of friends would go in search of excitement. The irony is that we took the money we stole from Santa's Village during the day only to spend it at another amusement carnival at night.

It was during one of these excursions to the fair that the Wacky Wire comes into play. There was a group of us about seven or eight large who decided to go and see what adventure we could get into. We were pretty buzzed up from the car ride's cooler full of beer that was accessible from the trunk by way of a folding backseat, and when we entered the gate, seeing the lights of the midway flashing gave off an otherworldly feel at dusk on this hot summer night. The rush of endorphins this brought made this time seem almost magical, and anticipation of what the night was to bring ran high.

There were dozens of different booths, designed to take money from the unsuspecting public, and seeing the shady characters running things I mentally imagined which of us would be doing the same thirty years in the future. After making wagers on who would swallow the live goldfish we won by throwing ping-pong balls into tiny bowls of dyed colored water, we worked our way down the Games Alley that put the one at Santa's Village to shame.

Bouncing around to the rock music blasting through the air, imagine our surprise when we saw our very own Wacky Wire game lit up brightly in the middle of everything. It was surrounded by people, throwing their money away—just like we saw earlier at the day job. With mouths watering at the chance to actually use the skills we got paid to practice all day, the four of us who knew how to win eagerly threw our dollar bills on the counter.

The shifty-looking Wacky Wire attendant was licking his chops at the sight of four obviously drunk kids with wallets full of money. The unfortunate guy had absolutely no idea what he was about to be in for. Kirk's obnoxious self always had to be the center of atten- tion so he stepped up to go first. Slapping the dollar down Kirk moved the wire hoop down the corkscrew with ease and expertly maneuvered it around the angled bottom. The red strobe light went off, signifying he won, and a cheer roared from the crowd. The game attendant gave us a look of shock and reluctantly took one of the huge bears off the back wall, and announced to the crowd on the microphone that he had a winner.

With the crowd growing larger by the minute, Dave was next to step up to the plate. He threw down a buck and proceeded to win a bear just as quick as Kirk before him. Giving each other high fives, the two were already pulling out another dollar to get in line and go again. Next up was a kid we'll call Dustin, a pretty boy with mop-top cut hair. Taking his lanky arms, he expertly worked the wire, and just as quick we had another winner. By this time the operator obviously realized he had run into a Games crew pack and started protesting. Realizing his job was on the line and most likely afraid of being accused by his bosses of selling the prizes, he was understandably ticked off. *"What the hell is going on here!"*

One of the kids that already won started smarting off that we all work at Santa's Village—*"Dude, we play this game all day!"* The operator started bitching and moaning about carney ethics, and started to refuse to let me play the game. *Are you kidding me?* With the booze fueling my anger, I wasn't about to let this fucker not give me my chance at carnival glory. *"That's discrimination, man! My dad's a mayor, and if you don't let me play you'll never have a job here again!"* Now my dad wasn't mayor of anything, but my loud antics were starting to cause a scene so he started to cave. After telling him that I'd stand there all night telling people the scam he was running, or better yet, I'd coach them on how to win—the guy begrudgingly took my dollar.

Now let's recap this series of events. I've drunk at least eight beers on the ride over. There are lights flashing, rides spinning, and a crowd of at least thirty people watching the spectacle I helped to create. My heart was pumping adrenaline from my yelling match, and adding to my nerves was a wave of fear rushing over me. *What if I don't win this?* I just saw three of my buddies win—including Kirk the Daring—*I can't possibly be the only putz not to win!*

As I grabbed the wand I immediately realize this was going to be harder than usual. My motor skills started diminishing before I even got there, and that was before I was so damn tense from all the stress. With all eyes on me I started my attack. I quickly brought the ring down past the midway point on my way to glory when suddenly my hand jerked. It set off the buzzer. *Shit.* The operator gave a smug chuckle, and the catcalls from my buddies behind me could be heard. Pissed, I pulled out another dollar and slapped it on the counter. With the rage of embarrassment encompassing me, I moved the ring down again, setting off the buzzer in quicker fashion than the first time.

I pulled out another dollar, and the crew behind me was starting to get restless. Complaining that their hands are getting tired holding onto their overstuffed bears made me pissed even more than I was already. I started again with the wand, and immediately set the buzzer off—not even a second into my descent. *Fuck!* I grabbed out another dollar, and by this time the crew said they're going to go on some rides. Determined to wipe the wicked smile off the game operator's face, I told them to go on without me. Twenty dollars later—I left with my head down in shame, bear-less and now being heckled by the attendant on the microphone for all to hear.

One of Jay Kramer's favorite memories was learning how to win Wacky Wire: *"We took the skills to Six Flags Great America—and won two huge cows and two big gorillas. All I had was my little convertible Cabriolet—and three girls to bring back with me. So we stuffed the gorillas in the trunk, and put two of the girls in the wells in the back, each with a cow. I converted the car, the heads of the cows resting on the roll bar, with the girls being straddled by them. We drive up to the toll booth and the lady turns around and falls over laughing. She screams to the other booths—look at these tits!*

*Another time I went to Great America with ten people, and we ended up winning eight gorillas and eight cows! All we had was one van. We got them all in there, but we locked the keys inside—we ended up having to give several animals to the locksmith as payment."*

**D**ave Decker also recalled the time the skills learned working the Wacky Wire were put to good use: *"I remember when a bunch of us went to Great America and wouldn't you know—they had the Wacky Wire. So we all line up, there were probably five of us, and we all pointed to the prize we wanted. Moments later—we all hit it. Beeps are going off everywhere. They're freaking out! Security came—everyone came—and they're like—what's going on here? We work at Santa's Village suckers!—and all walk away with these big ass cows. Later on we're in the parking lot trying to sell the things for like forty bucks. Security got wind of it though and kicked us out. One of us had a party later where we ended up tearing one up Lord of the Flies style—we mutilated a cow!"*

# I Could Be Such An Ass

## BY CHRISTOPHER DEARMAN

**A**fter my time working at Santa's Village came to an end about halfway through my second season—which we'll get into more detail later—the park continued to play a big part in that summer's fun. Being that I had friends who still worked there, including a girl I had just started dating (along with the many other females I was still trying to get to know), it wasn't uncommon to find me hanging out in the parking lot or venturing into the park itself from time to time. This was made possible rather easily by either sneaking in, or just using some of the many passes I acquired by dubious means during my time working there. It was on one of these occasions where I made a complete ass out of myself—in more ways than one.

I was relatively new to the whole relationship thing, and I really didn't have much experience on how to end them. My maturity level at the time was definitely lacking, and instead of being able to explain that things weren't working out like an adult, I generally would just ignore the situation and hope it would go away. It was either that, or act in a way where I would make them get fed up with me, and in turn, have them be the one to end things (a technique I've used often throughout the years).

This particular story I'm about to tell is one I still feel bad about to this day. It was the time I came up with the brilliant plan to bring a girl I wanted to date to the park in order to help facilitate my intentions of ending the relationship with another girl. Not wanting to deal with the confrontation of having to break up with this very sweet girl to her face, I had the bright idea to bring a date to the park while she was working, in hopes that my girlfriend would just get the hint that I wanted to move on. I figured she would see the two of us together and want nothing to do with me—circumventing the whole awkward verbal confrontation that was sure to happen, if I had broken up with her by traditional means. Trust me, typing out that memory right now doesn't make me feel the greatest, but what can I say, I had a lot to learn when it came to women.

So I ask this good-looking girl who worked with me at my new job at the Spring Hill Theater if she wanted to spend the day at

Santa's Village. Working on her ego, I told her that my presence inside the park with such a hot chick like herself would cause a stir with my former employees and get everyone talking. She would also be doing me a favor by helping me end my relationship with my girlfriend.

The weekend came, and the hot chick and I went to the park with some pilfered free tickets—damn if I was actually going to spend money to get into the place. It was a beautiful day, my date looked great, and I was soon going to be a free man. Once inside, I quickly realized I was also free to do something else I didn't consider when devising my "brilliant" break-up plan. Since I was in the park as supposedly a paying customer rather then employee, I would now get a chance to actually win at the Wacky Wire!

The chance to make up for my Kane County Fair Wacky Wire failure was even more exciting than being seen with the hottie. I rushed over to the game and slapped down a dollar. Thoughts raced through my head of how cool it would be to walk down Games Alley with a hot chick on one arm and a huge stuffed animal in the other. The added bonus to all of this would be that my girlfriend would want nothing to do with me, and I could then try to get with the hottie without being labeled a cheater. Thinking I could impress my date by winning her a huge prize, I confidently declared that she could have whatever she desired in a matter of moments. But before I could even pick up the wand, the girl working the game threw my dollar right back at me:

*"You can't play!"*—she said snootily, giving me a disgusted look.

*"Why the fuck not? I don't work here!"*—I said, furious at the nerve of this chick.

She was a friend of my girlfriend, and definitely didn't appreciate the fact that I was embarrassing her. I can see why she acted this way now, but at the time I wasn't going to let this bitch deny me my glory—I wasn't leaving until I won me one of the giant animals! So, I verbally went to town on this girl, reading her the riot act until she ended up calling for the Games manager. He soon came walking over to the game with a suspicious look on his face:

*"What are you doing here, Chris? You aren't supposed to be here."*

*"I'm a customer! Are you going to discriminate against a paying customer! I'll sue you so quick..."*

At the time I would threaten to sue just about anyone and everyone—like I had a lawyer on call or something. My parents had to have heard my threats to sue dozens of times when I was faced with a perceived wrong and knew I didn't have the means to actually ever do so, but this manager apparently didn't know better. After unsuccessfully trying to defuse the situation, he got on his walkie-talkie with upper management to find out how he should handle things. Pissed that I wasn't getting the opportunity to shine, I started mocking him for being a grown man not having the balls to make a decision on his own.

Various employees heard about my presence at the park, and started to crowd around the Wacky Wire game. No one wanted to miss the spectacle a former employee was about make. People were chiming in with their two cents, some saying I shouldn't be allowed to play (mostly the friends of my girlfriend who were pissed I brought a date), and others saying I should have my chance to win (mostly the ones who would want to try the same thing in my position). Finally, the Games manager got word that Management has deemed me eligible to try three times, and three times only—but that I can only win one prize. Where they got that number I don't know, but I was pumped that I would at least have my chance at Wacky Wire redemption.

Pissed at all the semantics, but confident the three chances were more then enough to conquer it once and for all, I agreed to the terms and slapped a buck on the counter. The attendant was still acting like a bitch towards me, and told me to my face she hoped I would lose. Grabbing the wand, and not having booze in my veins like at the fair, my confidence was beaming. I quickly brought the stick to the bottom with ease, and patiently waited for the right time to overtake the dreaded right angle. Just as I was making the final turn, I bumped into the side, and the buzzer went off like a knife to my heart. My first try was a bust.

During this time some of the other white shirt managers made their way over to the game after hearing on the walkie-talkies of the former employee who was attempting to get one over on the park. With nerves slowly starting to build in me, I slapped another buck on the table for my second try—and I quickly repeated the exact same scenario. I was choking under the pressure. The Wacky Wire gods once again were getting the best of me.

I took a moment to regroup, and then grabbed the wand for my third and final time. While words of encouragement from most of the guy employees was loud and boisterous, I was also getting words of discouragement from most of the girl employees, along with the dirty looks they gave me after realizing what I was up to. These looks were also aimed at my date, who at this point was getting quite embarrassed, and I could tell just wanted to get the hell out of there.

So with sweat dripping from my brow and the hopes of redemption riding on my shoulders, I finally started my descent. As you can probably guess—I blew it yet again. The pressure had gotten to me, and now most everyone was laughing in my direction. The guys told me that they would have won easily, and the girls told me I got exactly what I deserved. The Games manager gave me a fuck you smirk from off to the side, and walked away gloating at my failure. My date says we should hurry up and get to the matter at hand—in reality, she just wanted to get away from all the embarrassment.

Even though this was the case, it still perked me up a bit. While I failed in my attempt to win a prize, I still had a much sexier one on my arm—one who hopefully would also be in my bed later. All it was going to take was a quick jaunt to the Coney Island area, flaunt my date in front of my girlfriend so she would realize our relationship was over from just the sight of her hotness, and all would quickly end without drama. Not surprisingly, the outcome didn't play out as smoothly as planned...

I'll spare everyone the ugly details of exactly what happened, but needless to say, I foolishly didn't think through the reality of what would happen when I embarrassed my girlfriend in front of all her peers—it wasn't pretty. I looked like such an asshole for parading another chick in front of this poor girl, and as a result, my date quickly felt that same way about me. At the end of the day I had no girlfriend, no hottie, and no Wacky Wire prize to boot. I could be such an ass.

As a footnote to all this Wacky Wireness—I must have done something to make up for being such an ass because Karma finally ended up letting me win some of the huge Wacky Wire prizes on multiple occasions. One of the times was when I took my senior year girlfriend to Great America the next summer, and I won not one, but two huge monkeys. Another time was at Universal Studios in Orlando where I won a couple of huge Foghorn Leghorns. I ended up giving them both to some random kids, walking in the park, and it felt great to see the kids' eyes light up at the sight of a stuffed animal bigger then they were. The parents of the kids weren't too happy at my act of kindness though; as I could tell they were dreading having to explain that there was no way they would be able to get them on the plane ride home.

# WHO WANTS TO CARRY AROUND A PURSE ALL DAY?

**W**orking in the Games Department made you get up close and personal with all walks of life, as one former employee can describe in detail: *"One thing I vividly remember is the RIDICULOUSLY sweaty money that came out of big, fat, inner-city black ladies' bras to pay for games!"*

# D'OH!

**J**ay Cramer recalls how working at the park made for creating life-long friends: *"Everyone wanted skeeball. It was air-conditioned, and all you did was hand out quarters. One morning a bunch of us were exhausted from partying the night before, and Tim Duckworth had to come in early to stock the dome with all the new stuffed animals—so he REALLY wanted skeeball. That morning meeting there was a contest to see who would be the one to get it. All you had to do was race to be the first one to bring back a Homer Simpson doll. I knew that Tim knew where it was so I followed him—and tackled him*

on his way back! This kid Eric ended up getting one while we were scuf-
fling, and won skeeball. Tim, so pissed off, jumped up and screamed
out: "Can I go see the medic?" Bob and Jason thought it was so funny
that they put us in Water Race game for the whole day. It was one of
the hottest, and you had to work the hardest. We ended up becoming
best friends out of it, and he has even stood up at both my weddings!"

# Don't Try This At Home

## By Christopher Dearman

**I**t was a beautiful day in the park, and on this particular day I chose to work the Poster Pitch game, as I often did, mostly due to the ease of working it. Poster Pitch was a simple, but highly profitable game for both the park—and its employees. You already know about the most common form of employee profitability, but this story describes a more creative way I figured out to make money while working at Santa's Village.

With Poster Pitch everyone was a winner, so you didn't have to do the typical begging and pleading to get customers to play the game. This was during my second season working, so the carnie act had gotten pretty old by this point, and I either chose games to work where I could make the most five-finger loot, or where I had to do as little actual work as possible. The day of this story falls into the latter.

Poster Pitch basically sold itself. Customers would pay a buck to throw a dart at a wall full of cheesy posters, and if you hit the poster you want—you got it. There was absolutely no skill involved, so basically patrons would be buying a poster for a buck that cost the park pennies in bulk. This made it one of the biggest money makers.

The Poster Pitch game was built into the Polar Dome around the corner from Games Alley, and you were basically on your own when working it. You had no other employees working next to you for conversation, which on slow days could be brutal. The only entertainment you got, besides the customers, had to come from your own imagination or creativity. During times like these it would be smart to try sneaking in a magazine or listening to a hidden Walkman to kill time. Working on your dart skills got old after awhile, so you had to get innovative. I once folded the posters into big paper airplanes, and had a contest to see which one could sail farthest.

One of my childhood hobbies was performing magic. I practiced it growing up, putting on shows for family members from time to time, but because I had reached the age that I was now more interested in the opposite sex, I was apt to keep this fact to myself. My childhood hobby of making things look different than they appeared did come in handy though, especially when making it seem like I was actually putting customer's money in the game's lock boxes. This story isn't about stealing though. This is about when I devised one of my greatest illusions, and of course, it was concocted to impress a female.

It came to fruition during one of the slow days when I was bored out of my mind and decided to get creative with the industrial stapler used to put up posters. If you're familiar with these types of staplers, you know the fun loud bang it makes when pulling the trigger. I used to act like I was in the Old West and shoot staples at poster faces on the wall, at Coke can targets, or even at fellow employees who happened to walk by—in pure disregard to possibly having one fly in someone's eye.

While playing around with the staple gun, I quickly found out that it made the same loud bang sound even when there were no staples in it. This discovery sparked the idea to use the gun to create an illusion as a way to impress a certain female employee named Becky that I had my eye on for a few weeks. She was a gambler, so I also figured I might be able earn a few bucks to boot by creating a unique betting opportunity. With all the discretionary income we had, gambling on all sorts of things was another vice many of the employees picked up. It was easy to get the action going by coming up with dares and challenges, so I figured I'd try to create an irresistible wager that was foolproof to lose.

After taking one of the dollar bills from my money belt, I bent a staple directly through the middle of George Washington's head, and then looped a piece of tape on the back. I emptied the staple gun of all staples, except one. Then I told a fellow employee that was walking by to inform Becky to see me on her next break for a wager I wanted to propose. Having the items already prepared, I anxiously awaited her arrival for the premiere performance of my hopefully profitable shock-inducing feat.

A short while later she arrived to the Poster Pitch corral, blonde hair bouncing in the sunlight, and I was ready to impress. A few other onlookers came to witness what I had up my sleeve, so the pressure was on. Waiting for the last of the customers to walk away, I pulled out the staple gun with a flourish, and stated my intentions: I would staple a one dollar bill to the middle of my forehead—for the right price.

To prove that the staple gun was indeed a working device, I

placed a poster on the wooden counter in front of me and force-fully pulled the trigger. The lone staple I had left in the gun shot into the wood proving its functionality with a loud bang, and it now stuck out menacingly from the board. Taking out the already stapled dollar bill with the tape on the back from my pocket, I carefully covered the evidence of tampering with my thumb, and put it up to my head. Quickly replacing my thumb with the front of the gun, I held the stapler in place, and again asked how much it was worth to see me pull the trigger.

They were obviously buying it so far, as all eyes were bulging in disbelief at what I was threatening to do. Becky doubted my boast, and stated it would be worth ten dollars to witness such a feat—not thinking I would actually go through with it. To her surprise I quickly accepted the bet, then started praying to myself that a staple didn't get stuck in the chamber. I could only hope that I wasn't about to shoot one straight through my skull—killing me instantly.

With all the dramatic flair of a professional performer, I got front and center, and put a look of concentration on my face. I started to count to three: One…the anticipation was building. Two…the look of fear was on Becky's face as she was about to witness an idiot maim himself for ten dollars. THREE…I pulled the trigger, and the loud bang went off. Becky let out a yelp as I staggered back like I just got hit with a baseball bat. With the gasps of those around us adding to the drama, I pulled the gun away to reveal the dollar bill – which was secretly stuck to my forehead with the tape. Making sure to give all a close up look, they saw the bent staple stuck in the bill, evidently embedded in my forehead. Becky reluctantly handed over the money and left with disgust, telling me that I was crazy. As she walked away a smile formed on my face for pulling off the masterful feat, which lasted for the rest of the day.

Later on that afternoon it eventually filtered down to me from others that Becky was calling bullshit, and that she didn't really think I put a staple in my head. Not wanting to have my historic performance go to waste, on my next break I took the long way around to First Aid in front of the park, so that I could avoid having her see me. Telling them I cut my finger, I had the nurse give me a Band-Aid, which I then placed in the middle of my forehead. I returned to the game, and the next time Becky came walking by she saw the "evidence" of the puncture in my forehead. She shook her head in disbelief, and once again told me I was crazy. I'm pretty sure my exploits didn't impress her enough to garner a date, but as for getting a big reaction from her, my mission was accomplished.

# Duck Pond

## By Christopher Dearman

**T**he Duck Pond was the game no one wanted to operate due to having to deal with a continuous stream of annoying kids all day. That said, towards the end of my second season I realized it was one that I relished getting. The reason for this was that after many months of having to yell out spiels in order to get people to play my game, I was so sick of begging for

business. I felt that it was beneath me, and that they weren't paying me enough to stand and shout all day in the hot sun. The one
thing that always held true about the Duck Pond was that because
it was so popular, absolutely no pimping of the game was necessary. There were many days toward the end where this mindless
activity was greatly welcomed.

All you had to do was collect quarters non-stop throughout the
day, and give little brats the cheap toy that corresponded with the
number underneath the duck they picked. While you did have to
deal with the grating parents who would always ask if their kid
could exchange the toy they won for one they actually wanted, the
power you got to wield over them made for great entertainment.
Depending on the hotness of the mom, or coolness of the dad, I
only allowed those who I deemed worthy to exchange prizes.

If someone gave me attitude or tried to guilt me into giving their
kid the toy they wanted, you could guarantee that I wouldn't allow
it—no matter how much they complained. For these people, my
lack of compassion made the irritated parents cough up quarter
after quarter, until their child either got their prized toy—or went
broke in the process. Countless times I witnessed parents having to
drag away their screaming kid who didn't get the balsa wood air-
plane, or a pink plastic Snagglepuss ring they wanted. More than
once I was even called an asshole for not giving something up!

Even though dealing with the endless kids and aggravating
parents got old rather quickly, since it was the only game that was
kept open until the park's close, there was the added bonus of not
having to go to the parking lot to clean up garbage. Having had
to play garbage picker for minimum wage many times over the
course of two seasons, figuring out the Duck Pond loophole in my
eyes was genius. After an eight hour day in the hot sun, picking
up trash was definitely the last thing I wanted to do.

# CHAPTER FOUR

# GROUNDS & OLD
# MCDONALD'S FARM

# ✪ OLD MCDONALD'S FARM ✪
# & GROUNDS MEMORIES

The more labor intensive jobs of the park came if you worked on Old McDonald's Farm or in the Grounds Department. Being someone who at the time was looking to do as little work as humanly possible, I personally don't have much to say about either, except that most of the employees I came across who worked in those departments had a very distinct smell—one that I imagine only multiple showers could cure.

Surprisingly, most of the former employees I spoke with had nothing but positive memories of their time working in these areas. I found that hard to believe, but from the sounds of it, good times were had by all.

**M**atthew "Oil Can" Sparks started working at Santa's Village in 1987. Having spent four summers working in Barns, Grounds & Rides—he would love to go back in time and freeze those years he worked there. He appreciated that the owners took their time to get to know their employees, and got to meet a lot of wonderful friends while working. Shockingly, he never had the experience of anyone getting sick on a ride while he was working it.

*"Santa's Village—AKA Satan's Village to some of the workers—was my first job I got on my own that I wasn't related to the boss. My favorite time was when I was working in the Barn with Debbie...who would help with the birth of goats every spring/summer, and take her arm and put it inside the goat to make sure all the babies were out."*

*"We had a 'welcome to the barn department' routine that all new people go through. It's always done at the end of the day after pick-ing the horses out from the rides. The person (victim) we are throwing in climbs up into the loft to throw hay down, then gets a full bucket of grain to pour over it. As the person goes for the bucket—that's when they're thrown in. Back in '87, Ron got me. He came out of nowhere and knocked me in!"*

**His favorite two horses were the Clydesdales that pulled the carousel ride, named Wimpy & Mark.**

*"One day when I was working the pony ride it was a slow day, and the worker on the carousel ride was sitting in one of the swing chairs. I whistled and said—Let's go Wimpy—and he went around and scared the female worker that was working it!"*

*"Mark would do tricks for a little bit of feed. I would unhook him on a slow day from the pony ride, and take him into the yard and have him stand up on his hind legs for the customers to see."*

**He also remembers a llama, and a very special donkey...**

*"We had a customer that let the llama loose one day, and it started to run around the yard! It got the horses worked up on the pony ride, and they started to run while kids were on it. The other two workers on the pony ride tried to stop them, while I went out to help corral the llama that was running loose around the yard—scaring all the customers!"*

*"We had a Mediterranean donkey named, Elizabeth. She was so smart—she could open the gate to her pen, and all the other pens inside the upper barn. Some days we would come in to get the place ready for business, and all the animals would be loose! One day when I was cleaning her pen out, I bent over to grab the bucket of lime, and she came over and put her head down on my back — she wouldn't let me up! I had to have another worker come over to distract her so I could stand up."*

**Donkeys weren't his only bad luck...**

*"In 1990, I worked in Rides. I was on the merry-go-round where at that time the operator had to go into the middle of the ride on uneven ground to turn it on. I stepped off the ride right into a hole, and twisted my ankle. I sprained it, and was out of work for a month."*

*"I also got hurt a couple times in the two summers I worked in the Barn Department. Once, a half-wild ferret that a co-worker brought in bit me—luckily I didn't need stitches. Another time was when we had the*

*horses get out of the lower barn. One of them kicked one of the boards of the fence one night, and most of the horses got loose. When I went down to the fence area to help fix the board, I went to step past where the nails were sticking out, but stepped right on top of one. It went through my shoe and into my foot! I had to go to the ER and get a tetanus shot. I was put on the sleigh ride for the rest of that day."*

**But even after all that...**

*"Santa's Village will always hold a special place in my heart because of the workers and the customers."*

# IT'S BEGINNING TO LOOK A LOT LIKE CHRISTMAS

**T**i'ara Wendt-Rozell worked on the farm for two summers, and recalled a few memories of her days working at **Santa's Village:** *"There were so many, but one that comes to mind was being thrown into the horse trough. It was a kind of welcome to the barn thing. I felt accepted. I remember witnessing Debbi delivering animal babies. Watching a baby animal come into the world was such an experience. I learned a lot that summer from Debbie and the animals. Sometimes I wish I could go back."*

**She also laughs at her choir leader skills:** *"Here's one for ya—getting people to sing Christmas songs on the sleigh ride in the middle of summer! I was so shocked the first time I got them to do that...I had a blast working there, and I loved the people that I worked with. All the people I worked with were awesome. I made a lot of great friendships that summer, and I still keep in touch with some of them. I love them all."*

# I THOUGHT CURIOSITY KILLED THE *CAT*

**A Barns employee remembers an unfortunate day when they had to put down a sheep:** *"Bored from sitting in her pen all day, a sheep got loose and made its way down to where the horses were kept. I don't know if she was looking for trouble, but evidently she did something to piss one off, because a horse took a bite of the poor sheep's nose —leaving most of it missing!"*

*"Having become infected, the sheep had to be wheeled down behind the lower barn to be put out of her misery. A hole was dug, and a couple of the managers from the Grounds Department came down and shot it in the head. The sheep was buried, but went out knowing that she had one last night of adventure."*

# SCRATCH & SNIFF

**W**hen one employee was asked to recall something about another department in the park, she had this to offer: *"Barns people—can you stand a few steps away from me? Ok, now take a few more. There you go. Now, what's important?"*

**A** Games employee was a little more blunt: *"I remember the farm—those guys were weird. They have a really unique smell—it's called shit!"*

**A**nother employee had this for an explanation: *"The people working on Barns- they had to work in the same intense heat we did—but had to do so with a bunch of animals!"*

**T**he smell of the animals wasn't the only horrific memory: *"We had to saw off the horn on one of the goats because he kept jabbing people!"*

**W**hile the Barns employees pretty much had to contain themselves to the stinky Old McDonald's Farm area, the Grounds Department had the benefit and freedom to roam the park at will, without having Management keeping its eye on them. They did have their own special set of nauseating circumstances that they had to deal with: faulty plumbing, disgusting dirty diapers, having to clean up Voban, and many other unpleasant things—but even though it took a particular type of person to put himself through that torture for the minimal wages the job paid, one former employee reminded me that the job did come with certain privileges: *"What we would do because we worked Grounds is have a case of beer hidden in the park, and then go off and sneak behind a grove of trees and just drink all afternoon! We'd take our shirts off, get a nice tan, and then go back down to go mow lawns, whack the weeds, drop off gravel, clean up garbage. We worked our asses off, but at least we got paid to drink!"*

**M**arc Schock recalls another benefit to working as an orange shirt: *"The park didn't run without the Grounds crew, and we saw a lot of crap. One of the perks to picking up little kids vomit and maggot-filled garbage bags was the fact the beer tappers were left on in the picnic grove every now and then—or so I heard."*

**J**ohn McMillin, a former member of the Grounds crew who worked his first job at Santa's Village for nearly four summers in the late eighties & early nineties. Those times presented some of the greatest memories of his life. *"I miss the park, the friends, and who I was back then. I worked with the United Morning Maintenance Men—or as we were known to everyone else..."Grounds". I will always remember the brotherhood among the*

Grounds crew. We were like a fraternity and we were always trying to help each other hook up."

**Besides the camaraderie, his time at Santa's Village provided other unique memories...** "There was this crazy redneck guy who was in his thirties that got a job working with us under our boss Tom. There was an altercation or something, and he got fired. When he did, he threatened Tom, and several times he was seen across the street in his car, peering at the park through his binoculars! He was really weird, but he always made us laugh because he was so crazy. He also had this saying how he would "bust 'em in da chops." We always used to say it after he was gone."

"One of the weirdest situations I found myself in was my first year at the park. A few of the Grounds crew and I were cleaning the Coney Island picnic grove until late. We could see the nearly empty parking lot. Suddenly, we saw the managers leaving, and realized they didn't realize we were still in the park—so we were locked in! At first it was pretty funny, but then we realized we couldn't get out. We eventually had to climb the fence to get out of the park."

**Mother Nature didn't even bother him while working...**

"I will always remember working the picnic grove during the over-crowded FOP Day. Some of the best FOP day's occurred during a nice down pouring of rain. Teams of two Grounds men would continue to circle the picnic grove, moving tables, changing trash, and just chatting with the crowds.

**He was also well fed, and even has mementos to this day...**

"I use to pig out on the pretzels, and on the early morning shifts, the

*Grounds crew would on occasion help ourselves to ice cream bars while sitting in the picnic groves of the Coney Island area."*

*"While cleaning the picnic grove the following morning after an event, I found two Old Style beer taps tossed aside. I took those suckers, and still have them packed away today!"*

# RISE & SHINE

**P**hil Wenz fondly recalls morning coffee with the Maintenance crew: *"They would call it 'Nick's Place'—I would get to Santa's House at six in the morning at the latest - starting coffee, mopping the floors and cleaning-up. Two or three of the Maintenance guys would come and park the EZgos in the back. One day the park's owner Mr. Wilson came by and saw all the EZgos lined up, and started yelling—What the hell is going on? No wonder nothing ever gets done around here!—and chased them away. He then ended up having a cup of coffee with me."*

# HERE I COME TO SAVE THE DAY

**B**ack in 1988, a Grounds employee remembered a day the crew was putting up the picnic tables in one of the groves. After setting up the last load, they started leaving the grove just as people were coming in. As they were going up the hill to get out, the flatbed got loose from the tractor and started rolling back down the hill! The crew jumped off, and starting chasing the trailer – having to yell at people to get out of the way. Fortunately, there was an unnamed hero that day – one that rescued a little girl right before the flatbed smashed into the tree that she was standing in front of!

W hile they might have been heroes to some, one bitter former Games employee I interviewed over a few drinks obviously didn't think so: *"At the season end parties, the Grounds guys, they'd always try to outdo everyone—because they were just dicks! I mean, they were assholes—they were ALL assholes—all a bunch of meatheads. Fuckers that would always fuck with ya. There was that one game, where you had a cage around you, and they would always come up and unhook your prizes. They would just keep fucking with ya. You're just like, you know what man, come on guys—go sweep up some cigarette butts or something— don't you have a garbage can to empty?*

# PACKED FULL OF VITAMINS & MINERALS

O ne guy recalls a fragrant summer on the Grounds crew: *"One of the most sickening smells I encountered was the one found in the picnic groves. I will never forget the vile liquid that would pour out of the garbage cans after baking in the hot sun all day. We branded this G-juice and don't even get me started on some of the devious things we used it for!"*

# WAX ON—WAX OFF

**A**ndy Esch worked in Grounds during the summers of 2003 and 2004. He remembers enjoying being able to go all around the park the entire day, allowing him to talk with people from all other departments—the Rides people, Games, Food, magicians, even security. It was his favorite job to date being that it was so damn fun: *"One Saturday in the morning we put a few extra coats of spray wax on the giant slide out front of Old McDonald's Farm and slid down it a few times each. You should have seen how fast we went!*

*"Even though Grounds entailed cleaning up garbage all day, and being summer with 90-100 degree temps for most of it—it (still) was the funnest job I've had yet because of the people who worked there, some of which I am still in contact with today."*

# CHAPTER FIVE

# RACING RAPIDS

# ✪ RACING RAPIDS MEMORIES ✪

In 1983, Santa's Village developed the ten acres north of the park into what was at the time Illinois' largest water park. Racing Rapids provided relief from the hot summers with waterslides, Go-Karts, a tube slide and the lazy river. The park could be enjoyed on its own, or with a combo ticket with Santa's Village where you could play in the sun, and then cool off in the water. The fact that it was downwind from the smells of nearby Old McDonald's Farm didn't stop the many thousands of people's enjoyment of it over the years. While not as famous or beloved as Santa's Village, Racing Rapids still provided its employees with many fun and entertaining memories that will never be forgotten.

## "Co-ed naked Twister Tube sliding— enough said!"

### - As stated by the self-proclaimed hottest girl at Racing Rapids

**T**.J. Lewis worked four seasons at Racing Rapids during his high school years. Before this, his first job was cleaning out stables at a horse barn when he was fourteen years old. From there he got a job at the local McDonald's – which lasted about four days. Deciding then that his fast food days were over for good, he applied for a job at Racing Rapids – which turned out to pretty much be his primary summer employment for the next four years.

*"I started out as an attendant, and later on I worked in the Environmental Department—picking up trash and mowing the lawn. I actually thought it was more fulfilling to work with the environmental part. You didn't have to deal with customers; didn't have any supervisors looking over your shoulder. I was out there mowing lawns, getting a tan, smoking cigarettes, meeting girls, jumping in the water when it was hot—it was fantastic!"*

*"Even though it was a great job, I rarely started working there from day one before the park opened. They would call every season to ask me back, and I would always be – I'll call you back, I'll call you back— putting it off as long as possible. I worked there for about fours years, give or take. Initially my summers would start elsewhere, but I always ended up back at Rapids."*

*"There were many reasons why I came back—the camaraderie, the education, the whole experience. Just waking up at like five in the morning, having to be there at 6 am to open – it instilled a job discipline. I learned a lot. It was mostly for the camaraderie though—getting to hang out with people your age – guys and girls."*

**Speaking of girls, would you consider yourself a player?**

*"I dated a few girls during my time at Racing Rapids, but I was more of the type of guy that kept girlfriends rather then just hooking up. The two serious girlfriends I had though were wonderful individuals, never have a bad thing to say about them, and pretty hot to boot – one was a dead ringer for a young Kim Basinger, the other a dead ringer for a young Kathy Ireland!"*

**Where did you find time to work! Let's get back to the water park for a minute – did you ever witness anybody drown?**

*"Never had a drowning, but we had a lot of young kids that would have seizures. They would be bouncing around, and it was our job to try and protect those persons – make sure they didn't hurt themselves."*

**So did the park provide training?**

*"I can't speak for all, but I can say for myself that they had me in CPR class. I was certified for CPR, and I could also assist the paramedics with bagging people, where if someone is not breathing, they would open an airway with a tube down their throat, and I would be off to the side with an airbag compressing air into the lungs. That was actually where I got my first experience in emergency medicine, and I now I work for a fire department."*

*"Speaking of emergencies, some of the biggest memories I have about working there was the amount of saves I was involved with. I had some really good saves there – I was always pulling someone out of a situation he or she got into."*

*"There was this one woman who had a heart condition. She was riding on one of the slides while I was working the splash pool. So*

*I'm standing in the splash pool, bored out of my mind, when I see this woman coming down the slide unconscious! I pulled her out of the water, because she went straight down to the bottom dead weight, dragged her out, but she wasn't breathing."*

*"We started CPR, working her right on the side of the splash pool until eventually the paramedics showed up. At that point I gave up the CPR and assisted with getting back her normal breathing. They eventually took her to the hospital, but I never found out if she was OK or not. She did regain consciousness before she left though, so I assume she lived, and I'm proud to have had a part of that."*

*"There were other instances of life-threatening situations. Sometimes kids, but usually adults, that we had to pull out of the water due to pre-existing medical conditions, usually brought on by over-exertion. Nothing as memorable as when I came through with CPR though—I think the main reason I was always hired back is that we did good with saves. I always strive to step up when it comes to help with life and safety situations."*

**I see how that could be fulfilling. Do you remember any other benefits of working at a water park?**

*"The sun-bleached bathing suits that all the Racing Rapids girls wore — it was a beautiful thing — you could see right through them!"*

**That certainly can be fulfilling too! Besides the eye candy, any other benefits?**

*"Well one of the biggest benefits was the money you found while working in the Lazy River. It would just be floating along there, and you would just snag it. I would find fives and tens floating down the river*

*all the time. I would scoop up change. I actually would come out with twenty maybe thirty bucks a night!"*

*"By my second year working there I knew it was good to work the lazy river during the second half of the day. At the end of the night we had to walk the whole track to make sure there were no leftover tubes or people, and I would make a couple extra laps just for the hell of it, especially on a Thursday or Friday night because you knew you were coming out with beer money! And it wasn't just beer money for yourself, because you were like the king of the world with all the extra disposable income. You could buy all your friends beer because I only needed a six pack. We'd end up going out to a huge bonfire in a cornfield in West Dundee, or Hampshire.*

### How about injuries, ever witness any?

*"Here's a memory from the one time I was hired before the season started, and one of the reasons why I never did so again. It was one of my first days there, and they had me clearing out the layers of oil at the bottom of the Bumper Boat pool. We drained the pool, then had to go in with high pressured washers to strip these layers of black oil that were four inches thick and just caked on. It was eighty degrees out, and we were wearing our bathing suits, flip flops and t-shirts — totally not in safety gear."*

*"There were three of us, cleaning out the basin of the Bumper Boats that was just covered in layers of oil, and somehow the two other guys got into a debate whether the power washer would actually cut skin. Now, here we were cleaning these layers of sediment and oil that's covering the concrete pool, literally stripping this stuff off in six inch vertical chunks. You can just imagine the strips of oil that are just lying*

around everywhere, undeniable proof that there was a lot of water pressure going on there."

"So they're going back and forth, one guy saying he doesn't think it can break skin; the other guy saying he think it would, until they finally decide to settle the argument. The guy that is the doubter went over, and by the way, did I tell you this was his very first day working there? So this newbie put his hand in front of the pressure washer, and the other guy turned it on. Immediately, the water came darting out and cut this poor kid's hand like a large steak knife! It was pretty bad, and he was just covered in blood. The water completely split the middle of his hand!"

"Now during this time I was off smoking a cigarette or something, and I come back to see him calmly standing there holding his arm at a ninety degree angle. Blood is dripping down to his elbow and I asked him—What the fuck did you just do?"

"After listening to about five minutes of him retelling the story, I suggested that he might want to go to First Aid. I think it ended being like twenty to twenty-five stitches or something. He left the park, and never returned back to Racing Rapids. He worked a good six strong hours, cleaning up the fucking Bumper Boat pool, and then he never returned. He missed out on the bleached bathing suits! I mean, he had the world in his palm – like an oyster – and it all ended with twenty-five stitches in his hand!

**Do you have any "Gone Wild" stories of working there?**

"The only thing that would be questionable would be that I would have friends that didn't work there sneak in and ride the Go-Karts. At times I would sneak ten to twenty friends into Racing Rapids during the day, and if I was working the Go-Karts I would let them run for like a half hour! I would get yelled at by a Supervisor – T.J. what are you doing? I noticed that you just let this crew go for a half hour, and there is a line now waiting forty-five minutes! And they're drinking beer out there — what the hell is that?"

**Any bad memories?**

"I just remember people leaving dirty diapers everywhere, or when kids would shit in the pool!"

**So how did your time at Racing Rapids end?**

"I just moved on. They asked me back every year. There was never a year that they didn't ask me back; they always offered me a position. If it was still open today, I could probably ask for a job and get it."

# CALGON—TAKE ME AWAY

**A** Racing Rapids employee remembered a blazing hot Thursday when she heard over the radio that the trash compactor was broken, and that there was no way that it would be fixed before Sunday. This meant nearly four days worth of garbage was going to bake in the hot August sun.

Sunday, when the new compactor was installed, as luck would have it—she, a Racing Rapids Manager, and three Grounds kids from Santa's Village had the task of taking the twenty foot long, by eight feet wide, by six foot high heap of garbage and put it into the new compactor: *"I've never smelled something so awful in my life. The maggots were everywhere, and the garbage juice got on every part of my body. It took us about forty-five minutes to an hour for us to get all of that grossness into the compactor, and it was awful the entire way—I have never, and will never, be that dirty/disgusting/gross/filthy, or foul again!"*

# WAS HE WEARING A TRENCH COAT?

**W**orking the Bumper Boats one afternoon, a female employee recalls the time a man in short shorts came into her section and sat down: *"He seemed like an every day kinda guy, just like everyone else in the park..."*

She didn't think too much of it until she crouched down to unhook his boat only to find that this man's 'little friend' was coming out to make an appearance: *"A one 'man' show just for me!"*

# HOCK-A-LOOGIE

**S**arah Novak, who worked at Racing Rapids, the Polar Dome, and occasionally at Santa's Village from 1992 to 1998, remembered a time sitting at the tables waiting for a morning meeting to begin. One of the Assistant Managers was joking around, dangling spit above her forehead while standing behind her. A bit too confident in his spit-dangling skills,

Sarah got a glob of spit splattered down on her head while she was looking up at him!

# ALADDIN'S CASTLE ANYONE?

O ne employee that spent her first three summers fighting a sun-burned blister on her forehead, took pleasure dancing "on post" (the spot between the two slides), and also enjoyed some of the other added benefits of working at **Racing Rapids**: *"I found lots of money when on water quality, and left with full pockets of quarters when I worked the locker section as a manager!"*

> "Racing Rapids was like a never-ending episode of Baywatch!"
> - Former lifeguard employee

# I JUST LOST MY LUNCH

W hen asked what was the weirdest thing she ever saw while working – one employee recalled something out of a horror show: *"There was a guy that had all these flesh-colored balls on his body the size of golf balls, if not bigger, and he was on the Go-Karts without a shirt, and they were BOUNCING—I was so glad I wasn't working on slides when he went down!"*

# WERE THEY SEEKING REFUGE FROM GUNFIRE AT MCGRAWS?

**W**hen asked about seeing any unusual occurrences, an employee remembered: *"I didn't see it, but hearing about the deer drinking from the splash pool."*

# FEEL THE BURN

**A**fter doing the same things day in & day out, many employees came up with interesting ways to keep themselves entertained: *"One day on a particularly boring day Management put it out there to some of our Grounds crew that we would pay fifty dollars to anyone who would drink sixteen ounces of jalapeno juice from the food stand. Two people took us up on the bet—the only two girls we had on the crew! Needless to say we allowed them to take the next day off, and boy did they need it!"*

# STILL THERE TILL THIS DAY

**O**ne former member of Management remembered the time a little after-hours exploration by a group led to ownership having to increase park operation expenses. After a monster storm closed the park, some of them decided to go on a hike behind Racing Rapids, and ended up in McGraw's Wildlife Refuge. Following a road for quite some time, they recognized that they should probably get back into the park before it got too dark. After more searching, they ended up finding the fence up by the Himalaya, but realized it had barbed wire on top. Not wanting to have to walk all the way back, someone threw a coat they happened to be wearing over the top to cover the barbed wire, and flipped over the fence: *"We then made our way back down to Racing Rapids, and went on our merry ways for the night. We didn't think too much about our escapades until the next morning when we heard over the radio security trying to figure out why there were six sets of muddy footprints coming down from the Himalaya...and that is why twenty-four hour security was created!"*

## WELL, WAS SHE?

**A** Racing Rapids employee remembered the time a guy pulled a mean prank: *"Once, some girl asked this guy to put sunscreen on her back. Well, to be funny—or a jackass—he wrote the word BITCH in the lotion, and that is exactly what was burned onto her back! The poor girl had to wear a t-shirt most of the summer."*

## SECOND-HAND SMOKE CAN'T BE THAT BAD FOR YOU...

**W** hen asked what was the least favorite job at the park, one employee had this to say: *"There were a few shitty job* details working at Racing Rapids. The worst was probably the Bumper Boats. They were oily, and dirty – and all day you were basically sucking down exhaust smoke!"

> ## "I once saw a huge pair of breasts 'bumped' out of a bathing suit on the Bumper Boats!"
> – Former Racing Rapids Employee

## AMISH PARADISE?

**O**ne would think that days could be spent checking out the eye-candy, but for one employee, that wasn't always the case: "*I remember there was a certain religion, or maybe they were Amish or something, and that they rented the park once a year. They were very adamant about what you were allowed to see on their women's bodies, and no males were permitted to work the attractions on these days. I remember standing off to the side watching these ladies go down. They were completely covered with this full body suit like something a one year old would wear, but it was made of either cotton, or a cotton-wool blend. It wasn't that flattering, to say the least. They just didn't want us boys to be able to see anything!*"

# MAYBE WEARING A BIKINI WOULD HAVE HELPED

**A** former female employee remembered her desire for bigger & better things: *"I remember when the two DJs from the Radio Station B96, Eddie & Jobo, came to the park to broadcast their show for the day. At the time it was sort of a big deal, and I was determined to get some free concert tickets. On my break I went over to see if I could score something substantial, figuring I had an "in" as an employee. I ended up only getting a flimsy key chain and bumper sticker—both of which ended up in the trash."*

# A BLAZE OF GLORY

**W** hen asked about any unique firings, one employee remembered: *"There was this one kid who was like the king of Racing Rapids at the time. Today I wouldn't be able to pick him out in a lineup, but back then he was like the ringleader of the group I hung out with. All the girls dug him, and he partied hard until the day he got fired."*

*"I still remember how he went out. One scorching hot summer day just got to him. He was sick of the place, and sick of all the bullshit. He grabbed one of the heavy inner tubes, thrust it over his head, and ran up onto the bridge that crossed over the Lazy River. Standing up there with the tube hanging over his head, he let out a primal scream, and*

*jumped right off into the river on top of the people floating by! People talked about that for years. That was the thing about the place, after a while you just got so fucking sick of it, but you also had it so fucking good – that was the paradox!"*

# CHAPTER SIX

# LOVE, LUST & LONGING

# ✪ LOVE, LUST & LONGING ✪

hen asked if he tried to get with as many people as possible while working at the park, one employee replied:

## "Wasn't that the whole point?"

While that thought may have rung true for many former employees, there were also those out looking for love—and not surprisingly many found it. Whether looking for something serious, or just wanting some fun for the evening, having literally hundreds of young kids all working in the hot summer heat understandably brought about many hormonally raging situations…

# GOTTA PLAY THE ODDS

**B**arbara Ulrich recalled her favorite Santa's Village memory: *"Flirting, flirting, flirting - with just about every male co-worker there!"*

**M**ark Bloomer recalled one of his favorite memories: *"Girls, girls, girls—they were everywhere! All those Game girls, Shops girls, it never got old. All the drama. Who wanged who. Ahhhh… it was its own world. Big part of growing up."*

**W**hen asked if Racing Rapids had any games like Santa's Village offered, one former employee replied: *"Nothing other then the gossip – he made out with her, she made out with him— those type of games."*

**O**ne of the Rides workers recalls a time she was asked to lend a hand at one of the restaurants: *"I worked in Concessions for one day to help out. I was supposed to bus the tables, but was so busy flirting with the cook I did a really lousy job. I think there was a reason they never asked me to help out again!"*

**A** Racing Rapids employee still has vivid images of his summers spent working on the slides: *"The women were fantastic! The Dundee Crown girls, the St. Ed girls – especially the girls that would come back to work year after year. I mean, after one season of working in the hot sun everyday, those orange bathing suits would turn damn near translucent! I fell for many girls back then just from the outline of their chest alone!"*

# A KISS IS JUST A KISS

**K**aren DeBias remembered the days back in the seventies of innocent fun: *"Sneaking in after-hours to the Paddle Boat ride with our dates, and "making out"—OK, back then it was ONLY kissing—on the grassy hillside!"*

**O**ne girl remembers being an equal opportunity kisser: *"I had a crush or two on a few managers. I remember making out with one manager in the back of Coney Island; also made out with a guy from Grounds; made out with a guy from Rides..."*

**M**aking out at the park was also experienced by former Grounds worker John McMillian: *"The women. My god, it was like the most beautiful young women all got jobs at Santa's Village and pranced around in their little blue shorts. It's no wonder the young men were all walking hormones! I remember dating the same girl for about three years, and she got a job at Santa's Village during my second summer tour. Well, I was a one woman man until one day buses of city kids came to the park and there was a very attractive young black girl about my age that started hitting on me. I could tell she was a little drunk. I don't know where or how she got the beer, but I told her I had a girlfriend—but she didn't seem to care. Needless to say, it was only a matter of time before we were making out pretty heavy by this little hidden bench near the Game area. Unfortunately, I didn't get to do too much because I was supposed to be working, but it was a very hot make out session with a girl from the city that I never got to know her name or see her again."*

# WERE THE REINDEER GROOMSMEN?

**W**hen asked if he knew of any romance being sparked at the park, **Phil Wenz recalled:** *"I know more then a few employees that met at the park and eventually got married. There were even a few weddings at the park. A couple of skaters got married on the ice in the Polar Dome, and even Santa Don Goers had his wedding reception in the Pixie Pantry."*

*"I wooed Shop girls daily with my charm & charisma."*

*- Former Game-O*

# GOT MILK?

**W**hile there definitely was romance, more often then not there was pure lust, as one former Grounds employee **remembers:** *"There was a young married redneck kid, and one day he was caught with this heavy Spanish woman down in the Grounds shop, fingering her! Needless to say he was fired, and from what I remember, he cried like a baby, too!"*

*"At one of the company parties a fellow Grounds worker and a Games girl went behind one of the buildings and she whipped her boob out. He sucked it right there!"*

# IS THAT A FLASHLIGHT IN YOUR POCKET?

**O**ne former employee was asked if her first sexual experience happened while working at the park: *"If, by first sexual experience you mean the first time a guy hugged me from behind and I could feel his hard-on on my back, then yes!"*

**S**peaking of erections, even though a former Racing Rapids employee who chose to remain nameless was falsely accused of having one on the job, he didn't let that stand in the way of young love: *"I was dating a young lady – great girl, and I remember one day I was working the Tube Slide where you had to stand around in the splash pool for hours. Now, the splash pool had to be only fifty degrees water – it was the coldest thing ever – I mean it would turn your fingernails blue! Everyone would cry when they got in there. The only time it was ever bearable is when we had a ninety-nine degree day or something, but if it was rainy or overcast, it was the worst thing ever."*

*"So I'm working the splash pool, I was eighteen years old at the time, and I had this extremely attractive supervisor that had to be about twenty-four to twenty-five years old. She was a school teacher that worked at Rapids during her summer breaks. I remember she wore these big Razor sunglasses, and whenever she took them off she looked like a raccoon! But she was hot."*

*"About a week earlier she had asked me out on a date, and I*

explained to her that I was caught up on my girlfriend – who happened to work at Racing Rapids, and I just didn't feel comfortable cheating on her, that it wouldn't be a good thing. I said I really appreciate you asking me out, and under normal circumstances if I wasn't dating a girl – I definitely would have taken you up on that, but it's just not something I'm going to do."

"So time goes on, and I get stuck working the splash pool like four days in a row, which was something you weren't supposed to do. So I'm working it, and these are wet, rainy days – the water was fifty degrees, and it dawns on me that this supervisor who I turned down her advances was torturing the hell out of me! She kept putting me in that damn splash pool!"

"The kicker comes on my fourth day working the thing when I get word that the general manager of the supervisors wants to see me. He calls me over, and tells me that he has to write me up – and that he's writing me up for having an erection! I say to him—you KNOW I didn't have an erection in the splash pool – its fifty degrees water! My dick was like turtle power, almost climbing back up in me! He states that he has to go by the supervisor's word and that if I wanted to continue employment there that I would have to start wearing a jock strap! Now this was totally bogus – I swear to god – and this guy is saying that I needed to wear a jock strap because my cock was hanging out! There was no way that I was going to sign something saying anything of the sort!"

"Well, we continued the discussion, and I found out that not only did the supervisor that asked me out on a date was the one demanding that I be written up, but at the same time she also wrote up my girlfriend that was working somewhere else in the park for wearing a sweatshirt that wasn't Racing Rapids conforming or some shit."

"So I turned the screws on him—Dude, if this is really what you think happened, even though I'm telling you what's going on here, then I think I should have an attorney talk to you on my behalf because this

is wrong—It's a long-drawn-out story, but my girlfriend and I both got
fired, but we were both asked back the next season—and the supervisor
was asked to leave."

### So tell me about the girlfriend – was she your first kiss?

"No, I didn't have my first kiss there—but I had a few first kisses there.
One of them was the girlfriend in question. I actually kissed her for the
first time at the park by the gates on the way out."

"She had a friend that came up to me in the middle of the day
and said—You know she really likes you.—Now earlier that day she
was nice enough to rub tanning oil on my shoulders, arms, and back.
Actually, I was working the infamous slash pool at the time! It was a
hot day, so it was a good day to be working the splash pool, and she
was working on the rotation with me. We knew each other; had talked
a few times at after-hours parties, but this was the first time I actually
worked directly with her. I thought she was attractive, but I have to
admit, once she touched me for that first time, I dropped like a bag of
bricks – I was in love!"

### Are you sure that's not when you got the erection?

"No, no—I did not get an erection! That whole thing took place later—
this was in May or June, the whole getting fired thing was in late
August."

### So she rubs up on you – and you fall in love...

"She asks if I'm going to this party, and this was in the morning, we
ended up getting separated, but we kind of crossed paths on breaks,
and I'm telling her that I definitely want to hang out later. I'll go home

and change, but definitely meet me at the gate before we leave to switch numbers."

"So the day goes on, and I can't wait. I make my way to my time-card, punch out, and then I go walk up to her. We look into each others eyes, she just put her hands on my waist, and it just happened – we kissed right away. There were people walking in and out, a couple people whistled, it was a nice kiss – I was on Cloud Nine for the next few months!"

## So what happened at the party?

"Actually, I met up with her at the party, and went back to her house that night. I had to sneak in the place because her father was home. We didn't have sex or anything, but just made a lot of noise messing around. The next morning she goes to sneak me out, and while we were walking her sister comes out and grabs me by the arm! Now, I should probably mention that the sister was another one of those first kisses I had while working at Racing Rapids, and this only happened a few weeks earlier, so for spite she was like—I want you to meet my father!"

"So she drags me into the living room, and I see this guy in his underwear reading a newspaper. She says: This is the guy that was making all that noise last night; this is your daughter's new boyfriend. All I could do is extend my hand and say—Nice to meet you."

"Thankfully my soon-to-be girlfriend comes in to save me. She tells her father that I wasn't the one making all that noise, and that I just stopped by this morning to take her to breakfast before her driver's test. The father wasn't sure what to think, so I just kept my mouth shut. We get outside, she gave me a kiss on the cheek and told me to take her to breakfast before her driver's test – and we dated for quite a while thereafter!"

# WHAT HAPPENS AT THE VILLAGE—
# STAYS AT THE VILLAGE
### (until someone writes a book about it)

**A**girl named Tricia, who worked Attractions, Water Quality, and as a part-time manager at Racing Rapids in the late nineties, looked back at her time spent working at Racing Rapids during the day getting a tan, and nights getting drunk at Bandito Barney's – as the best summers of her life. Proud member of the "Sex in the Village Club" – she recalled a time she got busy at the Polar Dome. *"I was playing Shots Around the World (the drinking game), and taking my boyfriend home to have sex was my excuse to get out of the game. One of my co-workers wasn't having it, so he threw me the keys to the locker room—I couldn't pass up the opportunity!"*

**B**ack in the summer of 1996, there was a girl whose first job was working in Costumes, and then Rides. She recalled the quickies she used to have on her breaks: *"When I was in the costumes area we had a room upstairs in the Polar Dome where we changed into and out of costume. The door had a lock of course, so nobody walked in while we were changing. Well, the year that I worked there so did my then boyfriend. Let's just say that over lunch times that room was used for a lot more than eating! It was the sight of many a "nooner". Over the whole summer season this happened pretty much daily, and nobody ever asked why we'd be coming down from there every day....."*

**O**thers also confessed to more then just making out:

* "I lost my virginity there–lost it to a Game-O!"

* "Skeeball! That's where everyone had sex. I know many of us that had sex in the back of the skeeball room. Entrance chicks; Shop chicks–the wooden balls weren't the only balls being thrown around there!"

* "My goal was to see how many games I could win at, except the prize I was trying to win wasn't a stupid stuffed animal–it was having sex in the game itself! You know those twenty minutes or so we had to get the game ready before the park opened? It lent itself perfectly to have a quickie before having to open the gate."

* "Sneaking off to the forest with a young lady while everyone else was picking up garbage in the picnic grove just made more sense to me. If I was going to get all sweaty & dirty, I might as well enjoy it!"

* "Lost my virginity to some chick I worked with up there. It was my first season there."

* "There was a window in the back where we could see the stage next door. On the stage were some flamboyant male dancers, and some girls with too much makeup and bitch bangs that were getting ready to go tour in

Germany. Two people on break hooked up, and did it doggie style while watching the show one day!"

* "The Santa's Village parking lot was notorious for backseat loving. I just felt bad for the employees that had to pick up all my used condoms!"

* "The picnic grove area is where I got all sorts of busy with the ladies-it was just too easy to ask a young lady to take a walk and end up fooling around."

* "I once tried to get head in the little house on top of the Tree Slide-got interrupted by some damn kid though!"

* "Getting a blow-job in the Pumpkin Coach was always nice!"

* "The Polar Dome had all sorts of places where you could get frisky with ladies-and I made it my goal to do it in all of them!"

* "You know that bed in Santa's House? You could say I definitely spread some 'holiday cheer' on there!"

* "A chick came all over Dave Dekker's shorts, and the Leads made him wear them around all day!"

> \* "I am not sure about all of the 'things' that happened on the couch in the Racing Rapids supervisors office, but there was no way this side of the Galaxy Coaster I would ever sit on it without some serious towels between me and the cushions. I would think it would glow like the sun under a black light!

## ONE OF MANY SANTA'S VILLAGE BABIES?

Sheli R. still has a connection to Santa's Village to this day: *"I met my ex-husband while I was running the Himalaya— and I never will forget that day. I now have a fourteen-year old son from him."*

# A First Date Disaster

### BY CHRISTOPHER DEARMAN

**B**eing that many of my breaks were spent in search of female employees to flirt with, I spent most of my free time exploring the various shops, concessions, and attractions to see all the possibilities Santa's Village had to offer. The park employed teenagers from pretty much all the area high schools, so it was like open hunting season trying to track down new faces. Attending a private school that maybe had sixty or so females in my class, having a virtual smorgasbord of woman at my disposal to flirt with kept this warm-blooded ball of hormones racing all the time.

During my first season, even though I constantly talked to any girl with a pretty face, I didn't pull the trigger to ask that many girls out. While I realize now that the fear of rejection was the primary reason, back then I tried to convince myself that it was due to not having my driver's license. I had to contend with bumming for rides, or one of my parents having to drive me places as I didn't turn sixteen until mid-August. There was one attempt early on to work within my vehicle restrictions, but that date definitely didn't turn out as I had hoped.

I had spent weeks planning on asking out this girl Lisa who worked at one of the concessions stands. Many breaks were spent trying to flirt with her through the food windows, or finding ways to accidentally run into her while she was on hers. We talked often, and I would leave each conversation trying to figure out a good reason to ask her out on a date. That opportunity finally came in the form of the movie, *Dick Tracy*.

Now, it is widely known that the movie itself was a disappointment, but at the time Disney was marketing it as the next big thing. They were selling t-shirts with a movie ticket printed on the front for admittance to the midnight premiere, and I had the fantastic plan that this was a big enough spectacle to finally work up the courage to ask out young Lisa.

The t-shirts in question cost like fifteen bucks apiece, and this was before I learned how to supplement my income by taking a cut from the games, so I was making a pretty decent investment that the t-shirt would literally be the ticket into this young girl's heart. I don't recall actually how I asked her, but I'm sure it was awkward, and most likely had me sweating profusely and stumbling over my words (like drunk, only sober). Evidently, she must have said yes, because I am now writing an embarrassing story about what took place.

Let me try to paint a picture of how I remember this particular evening playing out. It was a Friday night in June, a little after ten o'clock. I was looking like a fool, wearing a *Dick Tracy* movie ticket printed on my chest, riding in the passenger seat of a car – one that my *mother* is driving. She was trying to make small talk on the ride to Lisa's in attempt to calm my nerves, but I did not hear a word she said, as I got more and more nervous the closer we got to Carpentersville. I kept looking at the clock, fiddling with the radio, and constantly looking in the visor mirror.

Around 10:35, we pulled up to Lisa's house to pick up this girl I only know from a handful of five to ten minute interval conversations, and went up to the door. In my hands was the second *Dick Tracy* t-shirt that I had proudly purchased. It may not have been dinner and a movie, but what teenage girl wouldn't want a *Dick Tracy* t-shirt...

She came to the door. With my mom in the driveway with the car running, I handed over the shirt to my date. She held it up to look at it:

*"Do I really have to wear this?"* – she asked with disgust.

*"Um, ah...yeah, that's uh...that's how we get in."* I said, barely getting the words out.

The look on her face was one of loathing, as I'm sure at this point she has regretted the fact that she ever agreed to this nonsense, but she graciously offered to go back in to change. Not wanting to miss the spectacle of a midnight showing, I made my first mistake. OK, the first mistake was coming up with the stupid plan in the first place, but my second was telling her that we had no time and to just wear it over her clothing. She gives me a look of "*really*," but went ahead and struggled to pull the shirt over her hair that I'm sure she just spent the last hour styling.

She tried to force a smile, but it was obvious she knew she looked like a fool as well. I tried to comfort her by saying she could take it off after we got inside the theater, as I hurried her down the walkway to the car. Like a gentleman, I then opened the backseat door for her. This brought me to my third mistake—the fact that I closed it behind her, and proceeded to get in the *front* seat!

When I got in on the passenger side, my mom looked at me like an idiot for not getting in the backseat with Lisa, but she didn't say anything. She welcomed her into the car, and I'm sure Lisa was happy for the third party to help break up the awkwardness between the two of us. After a few minutes of my mom keeping Lisa talking, I could finally relax a little knowing that my date was indeed in the car, wearing the t-shirt, and we were on our way.

After a short drive we pulled into the Spring Hill Theater parking lot, and my mom went on to pull up right in front of the place. I hurriedly told her to come pick us up in a couple of hours, as this was way before cell phones, and got out of the car. I opened the door for Lisa, and then hastily shuffled her off to the end of the line. Thankfully, everyone else waiting was wearing the t-shirts, but I don't think that made Lisa feel any better.

After a period of awkward conversation standing in line, we finally got in the theater, and only then did I really start to calm down and act like my semi-charming self. I got her to laugh a bit, most likely at other people's expense, and by the time the movie started things seemed to be going pretty good. Unfortunately, things didn't stay that way.

I would like to be able to tell you if the movie was any good or even what it was about, but it turned out I fell asleep about ten minutes into it. I awoke two hours later to Lisa elbowing me in the side, trying to get me to wake up as the movie was over. Wiping crusts from my eyes, she informed me that I had been snoring throughout the movie—really loud—and that she tried to get me up a few times, but after awhile just had to act like we weren't together.

Still groggy from my well-timed nap, we walked outside and I spotted mom waiting. Once again I went to open the door for her – and once again I slammed it shut behind her. I ran around the other side of the car to get in the front passenger side when my mom, God bless her heart, finally spoke up: *"You know you can sit in the backseat with her."* Looking back at Lisa, I knew that any chance of salvaging anything with her was lost hours ago. I said I was good, and continued to get in the front seat. After a ride back to her place in silence, needless to say—there was no second date.

# KILLING BRAIN CELLS WILL DO THAT TO YOU

When asked if he dated anyone during his time working at Santa's Village, a Rides worker's memory was a little hazy: *"I think I may have dated someone's sister, but I can't remember. Man, we really should remember this kind of stuff—it wasn't that long ago – the college years must have been kind of hard on me!"*

# THE THINGS YOU DO FOR LOVE

O ne young lady would resort to great lengths to try and get the attention of a certain Ride-O. *"I have a story about two teenage girls spending an entire day on the Snowball ride because the guy running that ride was cute. Another time the same dude was running the Ferris Wheel, so we rode that ride all day as well! We looked him up in the phone book, and called him. My friend ended up having a phone romance with his brother for quite a few months!"*

> "Those summers were like the Dating Game - a different chick each week!"
>
> - Former Rides Employee

# King Of Wishful Thinking

### By Christopher Dearman

D uring my second summer working at Santa's Village, there was this cute girl named Sara who started working midway through the season. She had an amazing smile and wide eyes which brought an immediate crush on her at first sight, so I was determined to get to know her. I don't remember exactly how we struck up our first conversation, but she told me that she wasn't a local and actually was from a small town called Wauconda. When I asked her why she would work at the park when she lived so far away, she mentioned she was living nearby with her uncle for the summer, who happened to be the Concessions manager.

Being that she usually worked the food window by Santa's House, and as standard operating procedure was back in those days, I spent many of my breaks going up to her window trying to get to know her. After attempting to do some major flirting on a daily basis for many weeks, I could tell she was sort of digging me. The problem was that there was this small guy who worked with her who would always try to sabotage my efforts to score a date! I think his name was Vince (or maybe that was the name of the short guy on my little league baseball team). Anyway, this guy would *always* pop up whenever I managed to get to talk to Sara.

This especially bugged me because they worked together, and everyone thought this little guy and her would make a cute couple because they were the same height. He would always come up cock-blocking me whenever I got her alone, saying the manager was looking for her or that she was needed back at the concession window for some lame reason. I wanted to punt this little guy in the ass for messing with my game, but he had seniority over me, so there really wasn't much I could do without getting fired.

My crush on Sara went on for many weeks without finding the perfect opportunity to make my move. Back then I would always over analyze everything, scared of rejection, but whenever I worked up the courage to possibly ask her out, the short guy would always seem to interrupt me just before I got the words out.

After many missed opportunities I finally determined that I would not let this go on any longer, and decided the day had come to ask her out. I waited around all day for the clock to signify day's end, when I would then perfectly time my exit from the park with hers. Once my Game was closed for the day, I quickly went over to the Duck Pond which stayed open later. I chatted up one of my friends while secretly watching the door that she would have to come out to leave.

When the time had come, I saw her walk out in her tight black staff shirt, and I quickly raced over to "accidentally" bump into her. The smile on her face showed that she was happy to see me, and it gave me the courage to ask her out to a movie that upcoming Friday. I was confident that she would agree to the date, and it would be the start to a long and meaningful relationship. Unfortunately, that was not meant to be...

I would love to say that she accepted and this story has a happy ending, but standing there with my heart on my sleeve, she regrettably informed me that today was actually her last day working at the park! I guess she was moving back to Wauconda the next day, which back then seemed so far away—like it was in another state or something (when in reality it's less then twenty minutes away). Needless to say, I was crushed.

Dejected that I had waited so long to finally get the nerve to ask her out, I asked if she knew if she would be coming back to work next season. I honestly don't remember what her answer was, but I do remember that as I watched her walk away she turned back, flashed me that amazing smile one last time, but alas, I never saw her again.

I still remember getting in my car afterwards to drive home and the song *King of Wishful Thinking* from the Pretty Woman soundtrack was playing. The lyrics of the song seemed to go perfectly with what I was feeling at the time, and to this day, almost twenty years later, whenever that song comes on it immediately takes me back to those memories.

# LET'S GET READY TO RUMBLE

**A** former Racing Rapids employee remembered how dramatic things were back in the day when it came to the whole "young love" thing. *There was this summer where I was dating this girl, and it became known to me that her ex-boyfriend wanted to jump me in the Racing Rapids parking lot after my shift. Figuring I could hold my own against him, I went to my car after work, but it turns out he had brought a couple of friends along with him. I guess the plan was that they would beat me up while I just stood there. Well, lo and behold, it turned out that I knew a couple of these guys that he brought, and they all thought I wasn't a bad guy. After they stated that they didn't want to fight me, I told the ex-boyfriend that since your boys aren't going to jump in, and since we're both here anyway, that maybe you and I should go at it like men. I had heard that he physically abused my girlfriend in the past to the point she ended up in the hospital, so I was more than willing to give this a guy what was coming to him. Not surprisingly, he kind of backed down once he realized he was on his own. He didn't get his ass kicked, but the fact that he looked like a pussy in front of his boys might have hurt him more.*

# BETTER THAN A BURGER KING BATHROOM?

**S**peaking of parking lots, Beth V. got busted by the cops one night getting busy in her parents' car in the Santa's **Village one**: *"The officer said he was going to call our parents, but never did...at least I don't think he did!"*

"I'll never forget the amount of disgusting used condoms found in that parking lot!"

\- Former Santa's Village Employee

# Fate

## BY CHRISTOPHER DEARMAN

**O**ne of the more "magical" memories I have from my time working at Santa's Village was from the last day that the park was open my first season. Kids had already gone back to school after the summer break, attendance was slow, and the park went into hibernation mode by only keeping a few key rides and games open. I had worked in Games all summer, but since I recently turned sixteen I was all about volunteering to operate rides when the opportunity arose. When a Rides manager came to the Games meeting this particular morning asking for volunteers to help out, I jumped at the chance.

I had already figured out that I preferred the ease and entertainment value of working the Tarantula ride, so when my request to operate it was approved, I was more than happy to work it on this gloomy, overcast day. My happiness quickly went south as the bad weather ended up not helping the attendance one bit, and I was lucky if riders would come maybe once every hour—which made for quite a miserable afternoon.

Cursing myself for choosing a ride that was pretty much off in the corner by itself leaving me with no one to talk to, I longed for the hot summer days where the park was full of eye candy, as well as providing the opportunity to make some extra loot from my stealing ways. Now all I had to pass time was standing in the cold daydreaming, with the only excitement coming from sneaking cigarettes behind a tree to break up the boredom.

After many hours of miserably counting the minutes until I could get the hell out of there, I was contemplating faking an illness to leave early when two girls my age strolled up to the ride. One was a pretty cute looking redhead with bright eyes, but I didn't give her a second look, as her friend was absolutely one of the cutest things I had ever seen. She was a little thing, with bouncy blonde hair and baby blue eyes. Added to this was a nice rack to boot—so it was love at first sight! The fact that she was wearing a Dundee Crown Pom Squad jacket only put my puppy love over the top, since I was a sucker for pretty much any girl who wore short skirts and waved pom-poms.

Not having the balls to actually try and start a meaningful conversation with the two, I stuck to the standard ride spiel of making sure they strapped themselves in, and asking them if they wanted a tame or wild ride. Saying they wanted the latter, I went over to the control booth, and told them that since they were the only ones riding it to just give me a signal when they were ready to get off (now that I think about it, I might have subconsciously been hitting on them by using that wordage).

After several minutes of giving them the wild ride they asked for, they signaled that they were done. I stopped the ride and anxiously went to let them off. The redhead gave me a huge smile, while the blonde gave me a shy one. Imagining she must be dating the quarterback of the football team or something, I figured I wouldn't have a chance in hell—even if I did get the balls to ask her out. Watching her walk off into the distance I looked at my watch to see when my next break was, hoping it was soon so that I could accidentally bump into them somewhere else in the park. Being that the Tarantula was at the very far end, once you rode it people generally wouldn't be heading back your way to the area. Pissed that I didn't have another break for almost an hour, I figured she would be long gone by that time.

To my surprise, about ten minutes later the two girls came walking back up to me. *"Can't get enough huh?"*—I said, or something cheesy to that effect. They giggled, and I again gave them another ride on the menacing spider. After they left a second time I started bitching to myself about my replacement taking so long to come give me my break. When he finally arrived I asked if he saw the two, and we had a short discussion about the blonde's extreme hotness. Hoping to track her down in the allotted fifteen minutes I had, I figured it gave me just about enough time to make it to one side of the park and back. I tried to think of something clever to say if I indeed found her, so that she would hopefully ask for *my* phone number, as I knew I didn't have the guts to ask for hers.

I did my fast walking act through the near empty park but couldn't find them anywhere, only getting tired and sweaty for my efforts. I figured my blonde goddess crush was gone forever, and dejectedly made my way back to the ride. Seeing the disappointment on my face, my replacement laughed at my attempts to track her down, and told me that he was going to go find them and ask her out himself. I told him to fuck off, and went back to my post, the sweat on my body now freezing to my skin as I stood there.

Time was moving at a snail's pace as I did the bouncing in place thing to try and keep warm. After a half hour or so of acting like a damn pogo-stick, to my utter surprise they came back yet again! At this point our conversation had gotten more detailed then the standard ride-speak, but the redhead was doing most of the talking, so I was under the impression that she must have been the one digging me—just my luck. She wasn't unattractive, but compared to the blonde bombshell she was damn near invisible.

They ended up coming back a few more times throughout the afternoon, and while I was getting more and more confidence chatting them up, I still didn't have the cojones to make a move on my rapid crush. Sensing that I was never going to transition from our pleasantries to actually making plans to meet outside of work, they said that they were leaving for the day, and I watched them walk away. The girl of my dreams had unexpectedly come into my life, and walked out of it just as quickly. The only thing I had etched in my mind was her first name that I got from seeing it embroidered in red lettering on her blue Poms jacket—but by that time it might as well have been stitched into my heart.

Since it was the beginning of my Junior year of high school and I was not yet part of what I would consider the "in crowd" at St. Ed's—the opportunity to run into her at a party or something was slim to none. I was the guy who the year before dyed his hair jet black to look like Cory Feldman from the movie *Dream A Little Dream*, and wore a jeans jacket with Freddy Krueger airbrushed on the back, so needless to say my standing in the high school social crowd had yet to catch up to my more popular Santa's Village persona. Still, besides the fact that the odds of ever seeing her again were against me, I somehow knew that this girl was meant to be in my life.

A few weeks or so later I was hanging out at the mall with this skater kid name Jon. He was a kid who did his own thing, and was liked by pretty much everyone. He had a locker near mine, and I had a car, so we hung out once in awhile. While at the mall we stopped in at Spencer Gifts that sold all sorts of cool and unusual stuff, and while we were there Jon ended up buying this huge poster of *The Incredible Hulk*. Now, it wasn't the kind of poster that was rolled up in a cellophane tube, but the kind that was made for display, backed by cardboard. This thing was huge. Not thinking much of it at the time, the two of us started to leave the mall when wouldn't you know, I see my dream girl and the redhead walking my way!

Not even having time to think, the redhead came up to us and excitedly said hi. I think I managed to say a *"Hey, how you doing?"*—but I can't be positive. All I can remember is staring at the blonde vision next to her. Here was the girl that I had been pining for ever since I watched her walk away that cold day at the park, and all I could do was stand there damn near speechless. As I struggled to think of something cool to say, the redhead did most of the talking as usual. I still assumed that she was the one who wanted me—but in my eyes she had no chance. Even though she looked better than anyone I dated up until that point, there really was no comparison in my eyes to the girl standing next to her.

After a while things seemed to be going pretty smoothly. I managed a few jokes and had them laughing, and my crush even started to get involved in the conversation a bit. I had a huge smile on my face, and everything was going fantastic—until I heard one of them ask to see what Jon had in his bag. My heart dropped. *Please tell me this isn't happening.* I telepathically tried to tell Jon—*don't you dare show them*—but I watched in horror as he pulled out the huge green poster of the Hulk with a flourish, elated to show off his newest prized possession.

While standing there dying of embarrassment, my dream girl commented that she liked the color, obviously only saying so to be polite. Feeling like a tool I quickly came up with a reason to get the hell out of there, but in my head I knew that I had blown it—and once again I would only be left with an awkward memory.

In the days to come I often thought back to this latest encounter. The image of her still wearing that sexy blue Pom Squad jacket drove me wild, and I would daydream about how her first name would sound, coupled with my last. Determined to make up for the two failed attempts to win her heart, I racked my brain on how I could run into her again. Not content with having to wait for fate to do its thing, I thought long and hard until it finally dawned on me how easy it would be to see my dream girl—all I had to do was attend a Dundee Crown football game!

Not wanting to go on my own I tried calling up some Santa's Village employees who I knew went to Crown to see if I could go with them to a game, but no one had any interest in watching them play. Thinking outside the box, I finally called my cousin Brad who didn't go to Crown, but went to their rival Jacobs High School. I figured that since both were public schools in the same school district, they must play each other at least once. My fingers were crossed that this was indeed the case, because even though he was a year younger, he could at least be my ticket onto school grounds.

Luckily, I didn't have to wait too long for my opportunity. When I asked Brad if his school ever played Dundee Crown, it turned out that the two teams were playing each other that upcoming Friday! I had no interest in watching the game at all, but was bursting with excitement that I might get to see my dream girl again. I spent days leading up to the game trying to figure out exactly what to wear, what to say, and generally pray that I find a way to make another connection with her again. I was convinced that the third time would be the charm.

When the day finally arrived I woke with a sense of urgency, and just prayed for school not to drag. Counting the minutes to the final bell, I raced home after last period to get ready for the evening. After eagerly showering, I styled my hair, put on my best clothes, and topped the look off with my father's trench coat. Looking back on it now I must have looked like a damn pervert, but at the time I thought it was way cool—in my own misguided sense of style. I got in my car and went to pick up Brad and a couple of his friends that I had hung out with a time or two. Anticipation was beyond excitement. Tonight was going to be the night lifelong memories are made of—I could just feel it.

When we arrived at Jacob's Field, Brad wanted to go find some of his other friends who he knew would be sitting in the home section. Not having any interest in that, I impatiently scanned the opposite side of the field to see if I could find her. Seeing the silhouettes of the Pom Squad doing their thing, I begged Brad to come with me over to the visitors side. Not wanting to leave his friends, I told him he either had to go over with me for at least part of the game, or he'd have to find another way home. Begrudgingly, he convinced a few of the others to go with, and we started to walk the track surrounding the field over to the other side.

After walking in my trench coat like a wannabe James Dean

around the curve to where the squad was cheering, I scanned the dozen or so girls in the hopes of seeing her. Like something out of a movie, time stood still when I finally saw her. In the distance I saw my blonde desire shouting out some spirited cheer towards the stands, bouncing up and down not in the blue satin jacket that I've seen twice before, but a tight blue Pom outfit with a ridiculously short skirt. It made me crush on her 100 times harder.

After what seemed like an eternity we locked eyes, and to my surprise she started *running* up to the chain-link fence that separated us! Mesmerized by this unforeseen action—as well as the bouncing breasts that were trying to burst out of her tight Pom outfit, I suddenly forgot all the things I had planned to say. Here was the girl I was dreaming about for weeks, and she had a smile on her face that lit up the field. The best part was that her smile was due to the sight of me!

What took place when she got to the fence is a blur. I know our time talking was short because she had to get back to the group, but that didn't matter. I didn't end up asking her out as I planned, but I spent the rest of the night practically walking on air. It was only then, without the redheaded chick in sight, that I finally realized that she must have had the same feelings for me all along—the look on her face said it all.

The feelings of confidence that evening brought continued after that night, and as high school went on, I ended up gradually becoming more part of the "in-crowd." Other crushes came and went, and while I thought about my Santa's Village love from time to time, eventually the feelings that were once so strong faded. I did end up seeing her once again during the high school years, shopping at the Army Surplus store in South Elgin, but at that time I was dating another girl, and while I didn't even make an attempt to say hi, she still made my heart skip a beat.

While that was the last time I saw her during my high school years, I would be remiss if I didn't mention the postscript to this story. It turns out it *was* in the cards to actually encounter her again. A few years after high school I had come home from Southern Illinois University for summer break, and ended up getting a job working as a waiter at the now closed Cracker Barrel Restaurant in Elgin—guess who happened to work there.

It's funny how fate works, as even though the circumstances at the time weren't necessarily the greatest for beginning a relationship, we ended up becoming fast friends and eventually ended up dating for a couple years. As with many stories of young love this one doesn't have a fairy-tale ending, but to this day the story of love at first sight on that cold and dreary day at Santa's Village still holds a special place in my heart.

# CHAPTER SEVEN

# AFTER-HOURS, ACCIDENTS & URBAN LEGENDS

# ✪ AFTER-HOURS, ACCIDENTS ✪ & URBAN LEGENDS

ooking back at my summers at Santa's Village, for me and many others I talked to, the days and nights pretty much blended together. You spent the days working at the park, and more often than not, spent the nights hanging out with your fellow employees. It was only natural to make friends with the people you spent eight hours a day with, and group outings after-hours were the norm. Being kids at the time, there was just as much mischief that that took place at the park as there was outside it. This chapter collects the stories of both, as well as some of the colorful accidents and urban legends that are associated with the park and its employees.

**W**hile working with Phil Wenz on this book I always get nervous when it comes to asking about or admitting to some of the hijinx & debauchery that took place at the park over the years. I mean, I was basically talking face-to-face with Santa Claus, and the little kid in me has great trepidation when it comes to asking some of the more risqué questions. One question that brought a bit of anxiety was when I asked him if he knew about anyone getting frisky inside Santa's House:

*"I imagine, and I don't know this for a fact, as I heard rumors after I came to the park of the house being used during the winter months when the dome was open as a place to entertain such an idea. I kept pretty close tabs on the house when I came to the park and I think it stopped. I ended up taking out the bed in 1990 because it wasn't politically correct—I was twenty-eight or twenty-nine at the time— and it wasn't appropriate to have a bed where there were young ladies working. It also just became such a pain in the butt, because kids would come in and start jumping up and down on it. So when I did finally take the bed apart, it hadn't been moved in years—it was pretty disgusting!"*

### How bout anyone getting tipsy?

*"We had one mother that came in with two little girls—and she was sooo drunk. I mean she was rocked—it got to the point that she passed out in a chair! We had to have security come wake her up and take her away to First Aid."*

**Any other stories of negligent adults?**

*"There were probably some instances where parents would drop off their kids and not pick them up, that sort of deal. I do seem to recall lost kids. Some people would sometimes just drop their kids off at the gate and never pick them up!*

# WHIMSICAL FUN

**P**hil Wenz also remembered some of the more playful hijinx that took place at the park: *"Before the park opened there were times Hugh Wilson would take a ten dollar bill and attach fishing line to it. When a grounds keeper would walk by and try to grab it, he would pull it away—just sitting there laughing!"*

> ## "I once slipped a whoopee cushion under one of the managers!"
>
> ### - Former Games Employee

**A** former Games employee had his own playful way to act like a kid: *"Sometimes I would spend my breaks entertaining myself by spitting on the customers below, or dropping plastic parachute army guys that they used to give out as prizes at the Duck Pond off the Sky Ride!"*

# IS THIS TYPICALLY ON THE MENU?

**A** former Santa's Village Concessions worker admitted that saliva also was sometimes used as a special sauce: *"It wasn't me, but I knew two guys that would spit on burgers before cooking them!"*

**A** disgruntled employee remembered the time he used a similar technique to exact a little revenge on one of the **park owners that fired him**: *"After I was ceremoniously let go for reasons I won't discuss here, I got a job working the concession stand at a movie theater. One evening shortly after my dismissal, one of the park owners came to catch a flick with his wife. Still having a bit of animosity for how things went down, I took the opportunity when filling his large Coke to hack a nasty loogie into it! At first I did feel a little bad that his wife had to partake in the spit cocktail I created, but that quickly passed as I figured it was her fault for marrying the guy. I hope it was refreshing!"*

# HAVE A COKE & A SMILE

**W** hile on the subject of quenching thirst, one could do so free of charge if you were friends with the right people: *"I remember one of my friends used to get us free Coke from the vending* machine he was in charge of—like all the time. He would just be like dude here ya go—free Cokes for everyone! He was a bigger guy, also a big pot head. He always would try to get us laid by the girls he couldn't get, because basically he couldn't get any. He drove this huge car we called, The Blue Bomber. He would pick me up for work, give me rides to places, we'd smoke Marlboro Reds. I have no idea what happened to him. I wonder what that fuck'n kid is up to?"

# POP WASN'T THE ONLY BEVERAGE CONSUMED

**T**.J. Lewis, an employee for four seasons, recalled how his Racing Rapids career began: "I remember my first year there I was like sixteen years old, and every morning we would walk in with these big sippy bottles filled with orange juice and vodka. The funny thing is that this ritual started for me on my very first day working there! Let me explain. So I pull into the parking lot on my first day, and I see this cool-looking older kid sitting with the car door open. I didn't think much of it until I saw him tip a vodka bottle in the air, and start pouring it in three of these sippy bottles. He's just mixing these fucking things with orange juice and vodka right in the parking lot before going into work, not a care in the world."

"Now, you got to figure I have the bright orange bathing suit on, newest guy there, greenest of the green, walking in on my first day — and I don't know anybody. I see hot broads EVERYWHERE, and all I can pay attention to is this twenty-year old guy making screwdrivers in his front seat — he had ice in a bucket! So anyway, I'm walking by and he notices that I see him mixing these things so he calls me over. He's like—here take one of these—so I did, and now I'm sipping on a *screwdriver while walking into orientation—I didn't know what the hell to think! Turns out that I can actually say that I found myself with the right group of people from day one!"*

# THAT SURE WILL HELP SOOTHE THE PAIN

**A** former employee who wants to go by the Cotton Candy/ Popcorn Lady remembered some of the good ol' days: *"Having worked there for four summers, I'm a bit sad, but all good things must come to an end. I won't miss the HOT burn-your-butt silver slide near Santa's hut, but I will miss Coney Island—nothing better than a blue snow cone with beer!"*

# SOMETIMES CRIME DOES PAY

**C** hris Morgan, a former employee of Santa's Village, remembered the day a life lesson was learned: *"A sixteen-year-old, mullet-clad boy I used to work with came to work one day still drunk from a party in the woods the night before. He reeked of equal parts BO and booze. He arrived, wearing a dirty red work shirt, his blue shorts, and high-top sneakers, fully intending to complete his day. His boss called the owner over to assess the situation. Mr. Hankie determined the kid was in no condition to work."*

*"He was given a lecture on how important it is to honor his commitments, and commended him on making it in that day. Mr. Hankie pulled out a five dollar bill and gave it to (him)—saying he should at least be rewarded for his efforts, but to go home to sleep it off. Mr.*

*Hankie flashed his money clip in front of several employees to make sure everyone saw the lesson being taught. The kid not only got out of making funnel cakes that day, but was rewarded for his underage drinking and courage to come to work drunk—simply awesome!"*

# WHERE THE ELEPHANT NOW RESIDES

**S**eeing customers enjoy themselves all day drinking outdoors made many employees want to experience the same sensation at night after work. What better place to do so than at a beer garden just a few miles down the road. One employee remembered those times vividly: *"Bandito Barney's was really connected to Racing Rapids during my years working there. Looking back, I have to admit that those establishments go hand-in-hand. I was sixteen, seventeen or eighteen years old drinking at that bar. I get off work at Racing Rapids, changing into my street clothes, and somehow—for some reason – and I know Banditos' was extremely strict on carding people – but when I was that young I was somehow able to enter that establishment. Most likely due to the many fake IDs I acquired over the years, but I remember drinking there like I was a fucking sailor who was in on leave. Like I was out to sea for like six months and what the fuck – I'm back and I'm pounding them like it was nobody's business!*

# IT'S NOT WHAT YOU KNOW...IT'S WHO YOU KNOW

**A**nother former Racing Rapids employee recalled a certain kid who got privileges that only being the son of a police chief brings: *"There was this one good-looking kid that worked at Rapids that was the son of one of the local police chiefs, and because of this he thought his shit didn't stink. He got into more trouble, but got out of more trouble – than anyone I ever met! He would be at all the area festivals, drinking right in the middle of everything, beer bottle tipped high in the air with cops everywhere. They knew who he was; they knew how old he was and they weren't doing shit! He eventually got fired for being crazy drunk while working or something, and I believe he ended up getting one of the Racing Rapids girls pregnant!"*

# YOU MIGHT BE A REDNECK IF...

**E**mployees weren't the only ones who imbibed alcoholic beverages: *"There were drunk customers all the time! Usually a bunch of hillbillies that couldn't afford to go to Disney World—or a dentist. I remember this one time I had to intervene with this hick that was wasted and harassing his girlfriend. I honestly thought he was going to beat her ass in front of everyone! I usually would just leave unruly customers to security because they didn't pay me enough to care, but the girl was kinda cute, and I knew I could take him. So, after watching this guy get more and more vocal with his screaming at this poor girl, I finally had enough and got in his face. Getting between him and his girl, I told him he better lay off before I called the cops. He* *quickly shut up once he saw I meant business, but then the chick I was trying to rescue started yelling at ME for getting involved—trailer trash at its finest!*

## "Drinking at the Alpine lounge for free -for many, many hours!"

### - Remembered by a Former Polar Dome Worker

# DID THEY HAVE TO TAKE A BREATHALYZER?

**A** former Racing Rapids employee remembered turning a blind eye when it came to his buddies: *"There were a few times I would have friends get kicked out of there for letting them drink beers on the Go-Karts, which when confronted by Management, I always was quick to deny any knowing. I think a few of them were still banned from going till the day it closed!"*

# NAMES WITHHELD TO PROTECT THE USE OF CHEESY PICK-UP LINES

**A** Food Service worker back in the seventies recalled the day of on-the-job cocktails: *"The last day of work before I went off to college for my Junior year, my buddies from the Pumpkin*

*Coach got me very drunk on vodka and orange soda while I tried to wait tables in the restaurant. I remember the Barn manager came in to order lunch and asking me if we had mutton on the menu. "No," I said, to which he replied—"That's too bad, because I'd like a piece of EWE!"*

**S**anta's Village and drinking often went hand-in-hand, and one of the most horrible days to work was the yearly occurrence of when the Fraternal Order of Police would join in on the festivities and rent out the park – the dreaded FOP Day. Literally thousands of off-duty cops and their families would come for a day of fun – many would say *too much* fun. These would, without fail, occur on the summer's hottest days, and you definitely had to deal with the highest ratio of customers who were the drunkest. Here are some former employees' memories:

* "Those guys owned the park – the cops – they were assholes. We couldn't control them. They were bringing alcohol in places they weren't supposed to, but then again – so were we!"

* Those cops would get fall-down drunk! I guess it was their way to let loose because they weren't on duty, but man, mixing booze with cops that think they could do whatever they wanted was a nightmare."

* "The best was when I would ask each one of them if they wanted the special pulled pork sandwich that wasn't even on the menu. Get it? Pig!"

* "I remember FOP day. I remember it gave all the workers that were on the take an added little thrill when they would be stealing the money from the park while surrounded by thousands of asshole cops! We were actually stealing police money! Man, we either had huge balls back then, or were just complete idiots!"

* "In hindsight I remember we would sit there and try to keep them under control, and they would be like – you're a sixteen-year old kid – fuck you – I own a gun and a badge! What do you say to that? Especially when you're sitting there, waiting to get out to go to an underage drinking party!"

* "I learned very early on that the best day to call in sick was on FOP day. You just better come up with a really damn good excuse!"

* "The FOP days were a NIGHTMARE! There were so many damn people in the park – most of them cops - and they thought their shit didn't stink!"

* "FOP day = HELL"

# GUNS & PORNO

**S**peaking of guns, Chris Morgan remembered the time he actually found one: *"One day I discovered a gun and some bullets hidden away in a box on a top shelf near the bathroom! The boxes were filled with the contents of a desk that should have been in a more secure area, but they used this space for storage until they could find another place. We also found some porno magazines — which all the sixteen-year-old employees took a greater interest in than the gun!"*

**T**hen there were the ones that were snuck into the park by employees: *"Me and some other Rides managers would bring our pellet guns to work. They were those handgun-looking ones. We would shoot them behind the ghost town along the train route. One time we were reloading at the train station, and a guest saw one of us with the guns and told someone. We hear this radio call about some-one with a gun! I run and hide them under the train trestle, and as I walk back, see all these managers down by the train station looking for a gun. I play stupid. They're looking and looking. The whole time they were stepping on all these bb's we spilt on the ground. Funny as shit. They didn't find a thing!"*

# Scarred For Life– Part Two

## By Christopher Dearman

**A** **certain type of gun also came into play** when I permanently altered my body for the second time. Even after getting fired for reasons I'll get into later, I still hung out with the Santa's Village crew for the rest of that summer of my second season. We'd go shoot pool at Harold's Pool Hall by day, and find reasons to drink and party at night. This lifestyle of drinking, smoking, and debauchery had me on a constant rush, and I was always on the lookout for what my next step in adolescent rebellion would be. Having already pierced my body, the next step would be to obviously get a tattoo—and I decided my seventeenth birthday would be just the occasion to do so.

During that summer I had somehow become infatuated with the character of Fido Dido. Don't ask me why, but the squiggly cartoon character that was the spokesperson for 7-Up was something I wanted to permanently ink on my body at the time. I think it had something to do with his philosophy of—*never do today what you can put off till tomorrow*—that had somehow struck a cord with my inner laziness. I had mentioned the desire to get a tattoo to everyone, but was met with laughter and ridicule. After hearing this, any doubts I had of actually going through with it were quickly squashed. I was determined to "man up" and get something all of the people who were laughing didn't have the balls to do.

The day of my birthday came, and my plan of attack was set. Knowing I had to meet up with the guys later that evening at some house party, I decided to drive myself to the local tattoo parlor on the way, and then be the talk of the party when I arrived. This evidently sounded like a good plan at the time.

Now, the only other person I had known personally who had a tattoo my age was the local troublemaker kid who lived in my court. A girl once wrote a smiley face on his chest, and spur of the moment he got it permanently outlined in black ink. When asked where he got it done, he told me it only took less then a minute at Ray's Tattoo's in Elgin for twenty bucks. Being my desired Fido Dido face wasn't much larger then what he got, I figured the price would definitely be right (obviously not learning from my earlier mistake of getting my ear pierced for five dollars, that the cheap route might not be the best route when permanently altering your body).

So, I got in my car and drove to downtown Elgin. It wasn't exactly in the best of neighborhoods, but being it was still twilight I figured I would be safe. I parked on the side road next to Ray's, and quickly slammed a few beers in the car while working up the courage to actually go inside. The beers had two purposes – one, to calm the nerves, and two, to have an excuse if anyone made fun of my choice of tattoo: *"Look, I was drunk!"*

After polishing off the cans of Miller Lite, I got out of the car and climbed the stairs up into Ray's. By this point I was pretty terrified, but after all the talk I had made to everyone – I wasn't about to back down now. Inside the parlor, rock music was blaring, and it was completely empty, except for two burly looking guys. One was this huge, Hell's Angels beast of a man who I figured was "security," and the other guy – turned out he was Ray.

I can't really describe what Ray looked like, except to say you would know him when you saw him. If there was a role for a seedy tattoo parlor owner in a movie, he would have been perfect to play the part. He looked me up and down, probably wondering what the hell a punk like me was doing in this part of town, but when I told him I was thinking of getting a tattoo he was all business. I showed him a picture of Fido Dido that I had ripped out of a book, and handed it over to him.

*"How much would it cost to get this?"*—I asked nervously.

Ray looked at the picture; then at me; then at the picture again. He shrugged and then started laughing like I just requested the funniest thing in the world:

*"Shit, if you really want to get this thing I'll do it for thirty."*

Being that I was prepared to pay fifty, I figured it was meant to be. After handing over the cash he motioned for me to sit down— his maniacal laughter still piercing the air. I walked over to where he was pointing and, I shit you not, he was instructing me to sit down in a wooden electric chair—just like the ones they used for executions! Needless to say, this wasn't exactly what I needed to help calm the nerves.

I'll be honest; at this point I was definitely getting second thoughts and was tempted to bolt up out of the place. I think the only thing stopping me was when I played out how it would look if I ran, or visualized potentially what these two might do if I asked for my money back.

After playing out both scenarios, I figured I might as well just get it over with. Sitting in the chair, tightly squeezing the handles on the chair, I watched as Ray pulled out a Bic pen and quickly drew the Fido Dido head on my shoulder. He asked if that is what I wanted, and I barely looked at it as I told him to go ahead – body shaking as I mumbled out the words. I remembered him making a joke of how I reminded him of how he gets when he's in court – again, not the thing needed to help calm me down.

The rest of my time there is a blur. He literally got done with the tattoo in a matter of minutes, and surprisingly, the tattoo gun didn't hurt anywhere near as much as I thought it would. He pulled out some Kleenex and Scotch taped a square of it onto my arm. He mentioned something about rubbing it down with lotion every so many hours, but at this point my adrenaline was pumping, and I was overcome with a rush to get to the party to show it off. I ran out of the building never to return.

On the way to the party I kept peeking under the Kleenex to see what it looked like. It was only then that I noticed that Fido was not quite what it was supposed to look like—it had squiggly lines for hair instead of zig-zags, but at that point I didn't care. I had overcome my fears, and was now sporting a badge of courage that I just knew would get the adulation from girls and guys alike.

When I got to the party I had a huge smile plastered onto my face. I gathered everyone around, and proudly pulled up my shirt sleeve. While it got the hoots and hollers I was expecting, it quickly turned into a question and answer session:

*"Where did you get it?"* – Someone asked.

*"Um…Ray's Tattoos"* – I said, nervously.

*"RAY'S TATTOOS – are you kidding me!"*

*"No, why?"*– I asked defensively.

*"Everyone knows not to go to RAY'S – that place is sooooo dirty. I heard of a guy just last week that got Hepatitis C!"*

*"Shit, I heard of a girl that got AIDS!"*– Someone chimed in.

*"Yeah man, you might be fucked—Ray's been into court a dozen times for people suing him for contracting one thing or another. Did you at least watch to see if he used a new needle?"*

Now this is when I truly got scared. My dumb ass had no rec-ollection of whether Ray had used a new needle or not – it didn't even cross my mind to bother to look or ask. I'd be damned if I was going to admit that to these guys though.

*"Of course he used a new needle!"* – I said, not having any idea.

After hearing that, they backed off a bit, but from that day forward they still took daily shots at me for being stupid enough to go to Ray's "fine" establishment. While part of me knew that they were just busting my balls, the thought of possibly contracting a deadly disease weighed heavily on my mind. *I don't dare get a blood test, do I? What if it comes back positive? What would I tell my folks?*

Eventually my senior year began, and less time was spent with the Games crew. The novelty of having a tattoo diminished, and my mind started focusing on finding a girlfriend, blood disease be damned. Then came November 7, 1991 – the day Magic Johnson announced to the world that he contracted the AIDS virus. Before this, AIDS was just something everyone thought only affected drug users and homosexuals, but when a star like Magic got it – it really hit home.

Immediately all my fears and insecurities came flooding back. I just knew that my dumb ass probably caught it, and figured I would only have the six more years of life expectancy—if I was lucky. I took to praying to God to let me live until I have sex with at least a few more girls, as well as keep me alive long enough to see any new Stars Wars movies that would be made. I wasn't asking for too much, was I?

Years passed, and I still kept a running count in my head of how many years I may have to live. There was no way in hell I was going to take an AIDS test, and since I figured it would be far better off not knowing if I indeed had anything, I just kept a running count of how many years went by. If I made it to six years

I should be good, and if I made it to eight years I would be in the clear. Eighteen years later I'm sitting here writing this book, so I'm hoping that's still the case!

# I Could Be Such An Ass–Part Two

## By Christopher Dearman

**L**ooking back on my days at Santa's Village as an adult, there are many regrets I have from my time working there. Stealing from the games, not having the balls to ask out my many crushes, getting a tattoo at a shady establishment, etc.—were all things I wish I would have done differently. My biggest regret though had to be the time I made a fellow employee cry.

In my defense, I did this strictly for the amusement of the fairer sex, but that doesn't make it right. It was during my first season, and John the Games manager graciously decided to have an after-hours roller skating party at this run down skating rink he owned out in the middle of nowhere. Most of us did not have means of transportation at the time, so John offered a ride in his van to anyone who needed one.

So, the night in question, my parents dropped me off at the

Santa's Village parking lot where I met up with eight or so other Games employees who were going to squeeze into the van. John was there, and eventually we packed his van full of eager guys and girls ready to go get our skate on. My crush at this particular time was a new girl to the department who had the nickname, "Strawberry"—I wasn't exactly sure how she got the moniker, but one of the rumors was that it was devised after a Ride-O ate the said fruit from her nether regions. At the time this rumor made me want to see if she had some fruit salad left over for me, as she had looked like a young Michelle Pfeiffer from *Grease 2*, a look that I found myself absolutely head over heels for.

So, after we all piled in the back of this big ol' van, I sat in the back next to my Pink Lady, and settled in for the ride. Being it was at night, and not having any lights in the back, it made for an interesting environment. Not really knowing how to pick up on my crush, I decided to hopefully get her to like me by making fun of one of the dorkier kids of the group. I can't remember exactly what was said, and I'm pretty sure I would hate myself if I did, but I guess I really laid into the poor guy. Once I got the girls in the van laughing, it gave me a free pass to keep at it until finally it got to the point where John chimed in from the front, and asked who the "funny guy" was. I think he may have said something to the effect of—*"Take it easy there, Chris"*—but I was on a roll. The laughter of Strawberry was music to my ears, and I wasn't about to let up now.

Continuing my attack on this poor kid's sensitivity, I was unrelenting with my assault on his manhood. With the laughter of everyone surrounding me, I continued my rabid attack, up until I heard the distinct sound of crying. Not just a little sniffle or two, but full out bawling. He was sobbing like a little girl, and at that moment I finally realized what a dick I was being. Immediately I was overcome with a feeling of remorse, and when all the girls in the van huddled around to comfort him, I went from the life of the party—to just being an asshole.

For the rest of the ride I silently sat to myself. When we thankfully arrived at the skating facility everyone piled out, and I attempted to pull the kid aside to make a much-needed apology. Knowing the embarrassment I caused, he pretty much told me to fuck off in so many words. With tail between my legs, I kept my mouth shut for the rest of the evening. I watched as he skated around the track laughing and having a good time with all the girls—including my crush, as I counted the minutes until the night was over.

There is a side note to this story. Even though we continued our mutual dislike for each other throughout our time spent working together at Santa's Village, we eventually crossed paths later in life. You can say he ended up getting his "revenge" for the way I treated him all those years before, but that is a story for another book. I can say that we ended up making peace and being friendly to one another, but if you're reading this now, please accept my sincere apology for being such an immature ass that day in the van.

# QUEER EYE FOR THE STRAIGHT GUY

O ne former employee who associated with the management side of things, recalled that busting balls wasn't always done by just the younger workers: *"There were always little gags and shenanigans that Management would play on each other in staff meetings and behind the scenes. We had this office bulletin board where we would put notes on for each other, post messages about calls that we had taken and whatnot. Well, one day, one of us decided to liven things up and pull a prank on the Games Department manager. We came up with the idea that we would leave a message for him to call this 800 number—one that just happened to be one for a gay porn hotline! So later on that day we watched him pull the note, go into an office and dial the number. We were standing in the hallway trying to contain our laughter when we start overhearing him go into this normal conversation—yeah, that sounds good, call me tomorrow—handled it as cool as a cucumber, like nothing was out of the ordinary at all. After he hung up he left the office, and we scurried back in to take a look at the number. Thinking we must have written it down wrong or something, we called the number to see who he was talking to. Just then he came right back in the office and asked: What, are you guys queer or something? Threw it right back at us!"*

S peaking of those that may be a little different, one former employee forgot how to play nice with others: *"There was a kid from Elgin who I worked with who looked a lot like Doogie Howser, but embraced the "wigger" lifestyle. He wore the chains, faded his hair with the lines in the side, and spoke a little like the crew from NWA."*

*"One day I pushed record on the boom box and fucked up his mix tape that consisted of Vanilla Ice, Salt 'n Peppa, and the Humpty*

*Dance. I cut into a song, and dropped my voice every thirty seconds making comments about my feelings concerning "wiggers" and their poser lifestyle. He was more than disappointed when he discovered the edits, and was most unhappy about having to wait three hours with a tape deck next to the radio tuned to B96 to capture a clean copy of the songs."*

*"The situation came to a head in front of the park at 4:30pm one day while he was waiting for his ride to pick him up. We started a fist fight – ok, I started the fist fight by knocking his sideways hat off of his head. It was a pretty lame fight, but he scraped his knee and got a black eye. My knee hit the pavement, and it hurt for a few days."*

# BURNED RUBBER

**T**hat same pavement was the scene where many employees could be found anxious to leave once their shift ended—maybe a little too anxious: *"I remember squealing my tires out in the parking lot. It was this one time where I honestly thought one of the Leads told me I could go home. So I punched out, get in my Ford Probe, and get ready to leave. I got the music bumping, and one of the Leads comes up to my window and tells me he never said I could go. So I'm like—well I must have misunderstood you. I can go punch back in if you want.—and he's like—No, I'm just going to write you up!—So I just peel the fuck out, was like—Fuck you, you prick!—I would love to see him today. I bet I could take him!"*

# LISTEN, SODA—YOU & PONYBOY— IF THE FUZZ SHOW—YOU BEAT IT OUT OF HERE

**F**ighting was also something Brian Ruden remembers from his time working as a security supervisor for a few **years:** *"I saw many interesting things. Some of which should stay private. My favorite incident was when we rented out Racing Rapids to a local youth group after hours. There were some rival gang members. Two large fights broke out. One in Racing Rapids parking lot and the other in Santa's Village parking lot. Six surrounding police departments showed up to help us break it up. That was a fun way to end a twenty hour work day!"*

# Cougar Hunting With Billy Idol

## BY CHRISTOPHER DEARMAN

**T**he parking lot was also the starting point for another one of my Santa's Village related adventures. We've already mentioned that summers working at Santa's Village were made up of many "firsts" for countless employees—first jobs, first cars, firsts loves, first hangovers, etc. While many of these things were true for myself, another first that I got to experience was attending my first rock concert without the parents. Yes, seeing the Beach Boys at Popular Creek; Starship at the Illinois State Fair, along with random local groups at The Hemmens auditorium were fun, but I will always remember my first concert without parental supervision.

Having just turned sixteen two weeks earlier, I was sure my parents weren't too excited when I told them that the guy that pierced my ear and I saved up our money to buy tickets to see the man with the platinum blonde spiked hair perform at Alpine Valley. In actuality, we got the money for the tickets from working the Bozo Pitch game, but I kept that information to myself. I begged and pleaded for them to let me borrow my mom's new Monte Carlo for the ride, and bless their hearts they broke down and obliged.

Meeting up at the Santa's Village parking lot the afternoon of the show, the excitement was flowing through my veins. I had a couple dozen beers stowed away in a cooler that I was able to stockpile from parties my parents had thrown the months prior, and we had a pair of lawn seats to see the man with a famous sneer in our hands. We peeled out of the parking lot onto Route 25, jamming out to Billy Idol's latest CD, and our out-of-state road trip had officially begun.

There were two things that made the show unique. For one, the concert was the first show after the tragic helicopter accident that killed Stevie Ray Vaughan the day before, and two, it was the first tour Billy did after almost dying in a motorcycle accident earlier that year—the tour's name: *Charmed Life*

The details of the concert are foggy, due to having slammed the beers in the parking lot before the show, but the highlight had to be our quest to see how close to the stage we could get from our tickets on the lawn. Sneaking by security to get in the pavilion, we listened to Billy's rebel yell as we slowly worked our way down the aisles. Hopping over seats, we generally pushed and shoved our way towards the stage until we reached the sixth row. Realizing we could get no farther, we looked around to find ourselves right in the middle of a pack of middle-aged women wearing tight rock t-shirts and big hair. Though not really the type of girls we would hit on at the time, not wanting to leave the awesome up-close seats, we did our best to flirt with the bevy of cougars. At one point in the night we had them believing that we were twenty-one and were convinced we had a shot at bedding a few, but after not being able to answer questions like what year we graduated—as simple math skills went out the door many beers earlier—the door to get with older women slammed in our faces.

We ended up passing out in the Monte Carlo at a hotel parking lot. I'm not really sure how we made it there, but I vividly remember getting woken up at the crack of dawn by a Pakistani man yelling at us to get off the property before he called the cops. I groggily got behind the wheel with a smile, and took solace in the fact that I had survived my first "official" rock concert.

# TAKE ME OUT TO THE BALL GAME

Other after-work activities included time spent at the huge park in Carpentersville which was home to many after-hour softball games between the different Santa's Village departments. A former member of the Games staff recalled one of those instances: *"I remember the many softball games that took place at Carpenter Park. While most of the guys were out sweating their ass off in those department bragging-right competitions, I took the opportunity to flirt with all the young ladies that were watching."*

*"There was this one time I tried to be cool and do this trick where you would flip a lit cigarette in and out of your mouth with your tongue that I once saw done in a movie. I learned the hard way that you needed to do it when the cigarette was burned down to the butt, because when I tried to do it shortly after its being lit, I had to open my mouth so wide that I pulled a muscle! My mouth cramped up so much that I ended up burning my lip! I still remember the look she gave me like I was some sort of damn fool. Needless to say, all the good vibes I was getting earlier from her went out the window."*

---

**H**e wasn't the only one who remembered those Carpenter Park games:

* **"I met a guy at my first Santa's Village baseball game when I caught a fly ball to center field that no one expected a girl to be able to catch. He was very athletic and was suitably impressed, so we ended up dating off and on for the next four years. We were part of a big crowd of kids that would head up on weekends to Top Deck in Lake Geneva, where the drinking age was only eighteen, to listen to an oldies band called Doctor Bop and the Headliners."**

* **"One morning at work we got attacked by a water balloon barrage in the Polar Dome. We ended up doing a counter-attack at a department softball game!"**

* Toke, toke, pass. Toke, toke, pass. Smoking bowls in the hot summer sun while playing softball was always fun!'

* "I recall the underage drinking of wine coolers in the trees at Carpenter Park while watching the department softball games."

* "We would all have trunks full of beer keeping cold in coolers of ice. You'd see people running to their cars, slamming a brew, and then hurrying back for their turn to bat."

* "There were many drunken softball quagmires."

# Southern Comfort

## By Christopher Dearman

Speaking of drunken quagmires, another one of my own personal firsts, which I will *always* remember, recalls the time I tried the enticing elixir of Southern Comfort liquor for the first time. It just so happens that this memorable occasion coincided with one of the after-hour season's end parties thrown by Management.

Having worked all day in the hot sun, cleaning up the picnic grounds and setting up for the bash, anticipation was high for the season's yearly celebration. After making plans to meet up with friends in the parking lot later that evening, I raced home to shower and get myself looking good for the night's festivities. Knowing of the many hook-ups of parties past, the thought of having a night of no parental supervision, a live DJ playing music, along with the dancing and revelry surely to come, I anxiously waited for my buddy Mike to pick me up from my Parkwood home in Elgin to drive me to the party. Arriving shortly thereafter in his mother's Ford Tempo, I told my parents I would be sleeping over at Mike's, and we then raced to the Santa's Village parking lot to begin our adventure.

Earlier in the day we had given money to a couple of the Leads to secure beer, and while waiting for them to arrive, ran into one of my crushes at the time. Knowing she was one of my targets for the evening to finally make some progress in the getting-to-know-her department, I was happy to learn she was in an unusually bubbly and flirty mood. It was still daylight, so I figured she must be on her way to getting drunk—a welcome thought knowing that it would only make things even easier to attain my goal.

At this point our beer still had yet to arrive, and since I was desperately thirsty for any type of alcohol, I asked her what she was drinking. Standing between parked cars, she looked around, and then flashed open her purse to reveal a large bottle of Southern Comfort. Now, I had never tried SoCo before, but at that point I would have drunk gasoline if she was offering it. When she presented me with the opportunity for a few swigs, I gladly accepted.

Getting in the backseat of her car, Mike went off to look for our beer as she and I took turns passing the bottle. The taste was surprisingly sweet with a strong kick—but things quickly went smooth after the first few shots. Eager to get a buzz, I was doing two or three gulps for every one of hers. We sat in the car for quite a while, joking around, and were becoming more flirtatious the further the contents of the bottle disappeared. I figured I was well on my way to having my own party—in the backseat of her car.

All the liquor I was drinking was quickly creating its intended effect, and soon I was raving that the stuff was the greatest invention known to man. The contents of the bottle was like a magic potion that gave me the confidence of Don Juan, and a personality that was reeling my crush in like a trophy fish. The way things were going, the backseat would be rockin' in no time.

Mike eventually found his way back to us, and requested to get in the car to take a few shots for himself. Pissed about the interruption, I begrudgingly opened the car door to let him in. This was the beginning of my downfall. As I opened the door to get out, I stood up, and quickly realized my mistake. The booze hit me all at once, and right away my head started spinning. The magical elixir that I was raving about minutes before was now immediately hurling out of my mouth at a violent pace—all over the parking lot, splattering the object of my affection's car in the process.

Needless to say that this did little to impress her. She let out a piercing scream of disgust, and instantly started gagging at the sight of my stomach contents. Mike, not even getting the chance to get some drinks for himself, started bitching me out and begged me to pull it together. Security was making their rounds of the parking lot, and if I didn't straighten up we were about to get kicked out of the party before it even started.

Leaning on him for stability, we somehow got past entrance security at the gate of the picnic grove, and made it into the party. Not surprisingly, my crush stayed far away from me from that point on, surely trying to get the picture of my puke out of her mind in the process.

Once inside I got my second wind, and recall partaking in quite a few of the beers the Leads got for us that were somehow snuck in the party. The DJ blasted dance music throughout the grove, and a good time was being had by all. Sometime during the celebration I vaguely remember getting pulled by the collar, while acting a fool on the dance floor, by one of the owners who demanded me to answer—*"Are you straight boy!"* (straight meaning sober—not sexual orientation). For the rest of the night everyone who witnessed this told me I was in deep shit for getting caught while wasted, and had me thinking I was going to be fired the next day—which made me slam more beers in the process.

The rest of the evening is a haze. I must have ended up passing out in the Tempo, as I awoke to find Mike driving me home at sunup, all pissed off that I threw up in the backseat. He was racing me home, swearing at me the whole way, as he now needed to clean out his mom's car before he brought it back home.

Head still foggy from the night before, he dropped me off, and I went to shower and get ready for that day's work. Still feeling the effects from all the booze, I drove back to Santa's Village with a pit in my stomach, dreading the impending call to go to the owner's office—certain I was going to be fired.

Amazingly, the morning meeting went off without mention of the incident from Management. The other Games employees spent the time after the meeting telling stories of the fun that had taken place the night before, and busting my balls for my drunken actions. I let them continue to have fun at my expense, as all I wanted to do was get to my game and pray for the day to quickly be over without any confrontation. Unfortunately, this was not the case...

A couple of hours into my shift I saw the two Leads (the ones that had gotten the beer for us) walking down Games Alley in my direction. The fact that they were bringing a fellow Games employee with them did not bode well. They told me to hand over my money belt, and informed me that the owner wanted to see me in his office immediately. Having never been fired before, the pit that was in my stomach instantly got worse, and they began to escort me to my impending doom.

With sweat dripping from my brow, I asked them what they thought my chances were of staying employed. They said it didn't look good, but wished me luck. When we finally reached the front office, I was resigned to the embarrassing fact that my days of working at The Village were about to come to an end. Just as I was about to knock on the office door, I looked back and saw the two of them doubled over, cracking up laughing. I asked what the hell was going on, and in between their laughter they informed me that it was all a hoax. The owner never mentioned anything about last night's encounter, and they doubted he even knew who I was.

A wave of relief came over me. My job was still intact, and the only thing tarnished was my pride and reputation. I spent the rest of the day cussing them out for making me the butt of their mean, but looking back, highly clever prank. To this day, it only takes one sniff of Southern Comfort to bring back all the feelings of that day in the parking lot. As you may imagine—it's not something that I consume often.

**C**hoosing to imbibe at the season end parties was not limited to me alone.  Many former employees remember kicking back and getting loose...

* "I remember one season end party that was just a BLAST! I was sixteen years old, and there were a couple employees that I was partying with that were of age, and able to buy us alcohol. We were partying on Santa's Village grounds all night, everyone having a great time. As soon as the party was over though we got in the car, and were immediately pulled over by the East Dundee Police right there on Route 25 - almost like they were just waiting for us. I didn't end up getting in trouble, but there was a couple of people that got arrested for contributing to the delinquency of minors—for providing alcohol to me!"

* "There was this guy that was at the employee party, sitting in a tree naked! He was acting like a monkey, actually hanging on the tree, fuck'n a glory to behold! This was in front of everybody. Girls were screaming & yelling. It was dark out, but we could see him up there acting the fool. I'm pretty sure he was asked to leave."

* "I remember one of the season end parties thrown by Santa's Village in the picnic grove. There was this very large kid from Games—name forgotten—who could sing, and everybody goaded him into giving an

impromptu a cappella concert. He basically knocked our socks off singing these songs!"

✶ "At one of the season end parties there were a couple employees that had snuck in a whole cache of fireworks–Roman Candles, bottle rockets, etc. They spent the evening running around the picnic grove and dodging security while lighting the things off. I don't believe they ever got caught, but it definitely added to the festive mood!"

✶ "I remember getting drunk before the season end party. We went to the Catfish Club and got to-go vodka lemonades from one of the bartenders we knew there!"

✶ "The end of the summer was always the time when you could get into the most trouble. There was always a year end picnic when the park was closed and the employees had run of the park. I would compare it to the scene in "Caddyshack" when it was caddy day at the pool. The Grounds crew had never lost the talent show at the end of the evening, and the year I participated that record held."

✶ "I will always remember the drama when two of our "brothers" went to war. One of our supervisors Ryan betrayed our team for the talent show for the company party, and told another department what a bunch of the Grounds crew were going to do on stage. With the idea stolen—Jason, I don't remember his last name, just that he was the stud of the crew—confronted Ryan with a "Why did you fuck us?" and quickly it escalated to blows. Jason ended up performing as Marky Mark at the show!"

\* "There was the lip sync contest—Willie Nelson and Axel Rose, interrupted by Sir-Mix-A-Lot—need I say more?"

\* "I remember at my first season end party there was some drunk employee raging out of control shortly after the thing started. He was just throwing haymakers at anyone that moved! Eventually security got a hold of him and dragged him off to the barn or something until the cops came. I don't know if anyone got hurt, but it was a hell of a way to start a party!"

\* "I remember drinking jungle juice and some shit—yeah, we got fucked up at those end-of-the-year parties."

\* "We would rent this boat that would take us out onto Lake Michigan. It would be all the managers on one boat with an open bar. Half of us weren't even of age, but that didn't stop us. No one would be sober at the end of the night."

\* "Man, I wish I had a digital camera back then!"

# SHOULD HAVE STUCK WITH STILL LIFE OR LANDSCAPE

**W**hile digital cameras weren't around back in the day, Polaroid ones were, as one former employee remembered: *"Back in high school I had this major crush on a girl in my class for a few years. While I was pretty good friends with her, she had a boyfriend, and I never had the opportunity to ask her out — so fantasies were kept strictly to my imagination. One slow day at work I heard a rumor that a Rides worker was showing off Polaroids of his girlfriend — in shall we say — a posing while taking business into her own hands kind of way. At the time, seeing any girl in this situation would have been a welcome sight to my horny eyes, but even more so when it turns out that the Rides guy's girlfriend was my friend that I had the crush on!"*

*"I spent my lunch break, trying to track the guy down, but I never did get the chance to take a peek at the photos. Realizing now that it would basically have been contributing to child pornography, even though I was underage at the time, I'm sure glad I didn't. Turns out later that Karma dished back some proper payback on the kid, because as soon as the dude turned eighteen, the girl's parents had him busted for statutory rape!"*

**T**his brings me to one instance where I'm sure glad there were no cameras around...

# Fried Mushrooms

## By Christopher Dearman

The juvenile delinquent I was quickly becoming at Santa's Village continued into the "real world"- mainly at department and grocery stores. This is ironic to me, because a couple of summers earlier I was absolutely floored and disgusted when I went to Jewel with a couple older neighborhood chicks, and they literally would just open their purse and do a little shopping - forgoing the whole checking out part that law-abiding citizens normally do. What a difference a few years makes, as I was now doing exactly the same thing - minus the purse. Looking back, what had changed? After much deliberation, the primary reason I can come up with is - BOOZE! Once I'd broken the taboo rule of underage drinking, stealing quickly didn't come far behind - and the story I'm about to confess has elements of both.

The day in question started off at the park with me and this girl we'll call, "Marissa" working the Frog Bog game. She was a cute blonde who happened to be one of those cool older chicks, even though there was maybe only one year's difference in age. Back then, if someone wasn't in the same grade as you, kids who were maybe born only months earlier somehow felt so much older. Marissa had just recently started working a few weeks into my second season, and more than a few of the guys definitely sported a major crush immediately after seeing her. So when she agreed to work the Frog Bog game with me that morning, I was more than excited to operate the game where customers would slam a heavy mallet onto a metal contraption that would then hopefully fling a disgusting rubber frog onto a lily pad floating in a simulated pond.

Looking for ways to try and impress Marissa on our walk to the game, I decided that she seemed cool enough to let her in on the stealing most of us had been doing ever since the season before. We were old hats to the pilfering by now, and by this time we had pretty much figured out ways to rip-off most of the games. It was always fun to "talk shop" with others, trading hints and secrets, and having the opportunity to show this older chick that I had a bad-boy side seemed like a smart thing to do at the time.

Turns out my instincts were right. The minute I let her in on how much money some of us were pulling a day, her eyes lit up, and she definitely wanted in on the action. She told me that she found someone selling a fake ID that looked like her, but had recently bought a used white Ford Bronco, and had to spend all her money on it. If she could get at least twenty-five dollars by the end of the day, she would have an ID to use that night, and that we could both hang out later to try it. That was all I needed to hear. I basically scored a semi-date with the new chick, and all I had to do was make sure she snagged a small percentage of what I would usually net. This was gonna be too easy!

That day at work went by quickly. It was an extremely hot one, and I was having a blast, trying to flirt by splashing her with pond water. The excitement of the two of us pocketing the customer's money while working this absurd game was making for an exciting time, and surprisingly, I was getting a ton of flirtatious signals from her. Looking back on it now, I'm sure it was mostly due to enlightening her to the ways of easy money, but back then I didn't care. She actually gave me a purpose for my stealing; as I desperately wanted to help my new crush attain that fake ID any way I could—especially so we could go on our "date."

I can still remember the smile on her face after our shift when she counted out the wet dollar bills from her pocket, and informed me she had more than enough to get the ID. Turned out she had snagged close to a hundred on that busy day—actually taking in more then I did! She gave me hug, and asked for my phone number. Since she wanted to show off her new truck, we made plans for her to pick me up later that night.

Evening came and I still remember looking out the window, seeing her pull up in the new-to-her used white Ford Bronco. This being pre-OJ, only now does this bring an ironic smile to my face. I climbed into the passenger seat of the huge beast of a truck, and she asked what I thought of her purchase. She called it her, "Baby Bronco" in this childlike voice, and even though it looked like a piece of junk, I wasn't going to be the one to tell her. I lied and said it's a sweet ride, and elated at the compliment, she pulled out some airline bottles of vodka she swiped from her mother's liquor cabinet. Even though we were on the way to go buy liquor, I was more than thankful to have a little something to help calm the nerves.

Once we got on the road I asked her what she wanted to do that night. She mentioned a party that was being thrown by a fellow co-worker, and I tried hard to hide my disappointment. I of course had already known about the party, but didn't want to bring it up because everyone I knew from the park would be there, which would make it hard to get any alone time with Marissa. Not wanting to sound like a drag, I reluctantly agreed it might be cool to stop by for a bit, and slammed another airline bottle of booze in frustration.

By the time we got to Carpentersville from my Parkwood neighborhood on the east side of Elgin, we each had knocked back quite a few of the little vodkas. Having the tolerance of a sixteen-year-old, I was feeling pretty damn good. Cruising around all buzzed up with a chick you have a crush on, lights flashing in the night around you, made all the talking and laughing we did seem like something out of a movie. The flirtatious vibes from earlier were still going strong, and I was definitely thinking that if I played my cards right I might get a chance to get with her.

We eventually made our way to the Dominick's parking lot where we were going to attempt to purchase alcohol with her fake ID. Even though each of us had multiple twenty dollar bills that were changed in for all the singles we took earlier, I had graciously offered to pay for tonight's booze, since it was her fake ID that we were going to be using.

At this point I was still a bit nervous about trying to buy underage liquor, but with her being a year older, I figured she would be able to get the booze with no problem. She was all excited about her new fake ID, and the excitement of being with someone who had one rubbed off on me. I asked her to bust it out and let me see what our delinquent actions bought her. She handed it over with a flourish, and I grabbed it to take a closer look. Now, the ID was of a girl who happened to be twenty-one, but when Marissa asked if it looked like her, I had to lie with a straight face and say it did—knowing damn well it looked *nothing* like her. I could tell that deep down she knew this, and was just hoping that I would tell her otherwise. We sat there for a moment, debating the risks involved, and I could tell she was trying to convince herself that it would work as well.

The drinks at this point had certainly kicked in, and after working up enough courage we walked into Dominick's. We immediately started racing around the liquor aisles like children in a candy store. I never really went down these aisles with the intent to purchase before, so it was definitely an exhilarating feeling. We traversed the aisles for what seemed like forever, debating what to get, and I could tell that she was stalling. I tried to pump her up by saying it would work, but she first wanted to go over by the checkout area to try to determine which cashier was more likely to not have good eyesight.

Deciding that we should try to find an elderly cashier who hopefully couldn't see straight, we looked around, but to our dismay there were only two cashiers. One was a stern-looking parent type, and the other looked like he was still in high school, and definitely not of age. If we went to that line we would have to go through the process of his having to call a store manager to come verify the ID. Knowing that the chances of the manager being an easy mark after being interrupted from what he was doing was slim-to-none, especially one that was being held by two obviously underage looking kids, we decided to go back to the liquor aisle to regroup.

After getting back to the liquor section we tried to come up with a plan of attack. Once we wrapped up the drawn out process of concluding that we should keep vodka the drink of choice for the evening, we stood in front of the many options lined up before us. For some unknown reason, we decided getting a big ass bottle of Gordon's vodka would be a smart choice since it was the cheapest, not knowing that it would taste like toilet water.

Sick of wasting any more time at this grocery store when I'd much rather be at a house with bedrooms to occupy, I suggested we might as well try the stern parental type. If any drama happens—we just run! After thinking this over for a moment she decided she has a better idea (which might have been her original idea all along now that I think about it). She took the bottle, put it into her luggage-sized purse, and told me to go buy some gum.

Looking at her with astonishment, and now officially starting to get scared of getting caught, I started freaking out a bit. *"Marissa, you can see the bright-ass orange bottle cap hanging out of your purse. How the fuck you going to get out of the store with what looks to be a damn police flare sticking up out of it?"* She casually put the strap over her shoulder, cradling the actual purse in her hands, and then grabbed my arm and interlocked it with hers. *"We'll just act like we're boyfriend and girlfriend."*—needless to say, the heart rate jumped even more.

We worked our way towards the cashier and started acting like we were a couple. When we got to the register, she put her head on my shoulder to help conceal the bottle, and now on top of all the drama I was currently in, I had the task to try to contain the ever growing wood in my pants! Amazingly, we somehow got through the cash out process undetected, and made our way back to the Bronco. It felt like we just robbed Fort Knox, but we were now off to the party with a full bottle of booze. In my eyes, in the goal of getting with her tonight—I had just gotten a little closer to the prize.

Now there is one other detail to this story that I have failed to mention. There may have been an ulterior motive for her wanting to go to this particular party that evening. During the short time since she had started working she had mentioned to more then a few people that she had a crush on this kid Dave. He was a casual friend of mine who looked similar to me, but was admittedly even better looking. While I had the goofy good looks of not quite being finished with puberty, he already had the standard tall, dark and handsome look, and had pretty much called "dibs" on her when she first started.

So with trepidation that my "date" might now be ending, we made it to the party, and immediately I could tell that word had gotten back to Dave that Marissa liked him. I tried to hold my anger back when he cockily informed me he was going to get with her. Knowing this most likely would be the case—and something I absolutely didn't want happening—I stuck to Marissa most of the night. We had committed a caper together, and that bond was surprisingly strong. We sat around a table together doing shots of the disgusting Gordons and playing drinking games—the two of us quickly getting more drunk.

During a game of cards someone took orders to go pick up some food from Hoppe's Bar down the road. We ordered a huge spread of appetizers, as pretty much all of us had a ton of money from the daily burglary of the day job. We got all sorts of fried foods—potato skins, shrimp, poppers, and a personal favorite of mine at the time—fried mushrooms. Since everyone was drunk, we all devoured the grub almost immediately after it arrived. I personally had to have inhaled at least a dozen mushrooms.

The drinking games went on later into the evening and I don't know if Marissa was doing this to get Dave jealous, or if somehow she was falling for my great personality over the course of the last couple of hours, but she was basically continuing our Dominick's boyfriend and girlfriend act right there at the table. She was trying to tickle my side, whispering suggestive thoughts into my ear, and even grabbing at my crotch under the table. After a few times of this I finally got the hint and confidence to ask her into one of the bedrooms. Making up some excuse of wanting to tell her something private, we stumbled our way into one of the bedrooms where we found a huge waterbed. Looking like fun, we jumped on the bed with our now half empty bottle of Gordons and two shot glasses—and started to play some drinking games.

Not having the balls to make the first move on my older crush, and just being excited to finally be alone with her, I continued downing shots for any reason. The night is definitely foggy, but I'm pretty sure I was getting the signal that I was going to get with her.

At this point the moving of the waterbed—while fun at first—was now making the whole room dizzy. We laid down. I'm literally inches away from her. We were face to face. I was about to go in for the kiss, and then...BOOM—I start throwing up *all over* the place. All over her, all over the blankets, the bed, on the floor—I was like that chick from the movie *Exorcist* spewing pea soup!

Next thing I know, the bedroom door busted open flooding the room with light. A group of people had run into the room after hearing Marissa's yells, and the only other sound I heard is someone yelling out:

# "FUCK'N MUSHROOMS!"

The guy who I assume was having the party started getting in my face ready to beat my drunken blob of an ass, as I desperately tried to comprehend what was happening with me. He was screaming that his parents were going to kill him while I was busy moaning, trying to keep down the nausea. Dave's boys were also there, and all the while they were telling me—*"That's fucked up man, you know it was Dave's girl."*—and speak of the devil, I saw him taking Marissa by the hand and walking her out of the bedroom!

With my head still spinning, embarrassed, and extremely emotional about all the drama going on around me, I stormed out of the house and started walking back to my home in Parkwood. It was easily a few good miles, and with puke all over my clothes, I swore to myself—I'd never eat fried mushrooms again.

**W**hen interviewing a couple of people for this book and bringing up this particular night's activities, not surprisingly they still remembered this incident which took place almost twenty years earlier:

**MICHAEL REEVES:** *"I remember you throwing up the mushrooms— and I remember you didn't even chew them! I know this because in your puke they were all whole!"*

**DAVID DEKKER:** *"Tall, blonde, nice boobs. I think it was Brian's party—now this is coming back to me. Yeah, I think it was Brian's party. You puked; then you left, and then she started puking. I was in the bathroom with her—oh, you'll be ok—I was pulling back her hair, sort of groping her back, being that guy. I think you puked in his parent's bed. But no, I never hit it, I never did. She was so sick that I could have taken advantage of that, but you know what, no. She smells like puke, probably tastes like puke, I'll just let her sleep. She did drive me to work a few times after that. She had a great body, but I just couldn't do it—couldn't seal the deal—dammit!"*

**B**esides the regret of not ever getting with that particular blonde, Dave Dekker did have many stories of adolescent fun during his Santa's Village days. He again wants to stress to his friends, family and employers that all this happened a long time ago, and that he wouldn't dare do some of things he did back then now. He recalled some of the after-hours shenanigans that took place during those summers: *"Man, the parties we*

had—the after-hour parties were so great because we worked with this guy Jay whose parents had an in the ground pool, and we just partied over there all the time – even if nobody was home! I have pictures of me in a sombrero hat—in the pool—drinking Coors—at age sixteen!"

**For many, those times were the first time they experimented with marijuana. Did you partake?**

"My first time was when working at Santa's Village—it was actually at an apartment in Carpentersville where some of the Leads lived! We all just got fucked up – to the point that one of our buddies was humping the damn couch – that's how fucked up he was—and I'm sitting in the kitchen, staring at the window. I remember this so like it was yesterday – and I was sitting there, thinking that I was morphing into my dad! I'm like—oh my god—I look just like him! What's going on here?"

"Then immediately the munchies hit, and we just start EATING! This cute little redhead comes in, one of the Lead's girlfriends, and she's like—You guys must have the munchies—and we were like, hell yeah!"

"So after stuffing my face, I go smack the guy in the living room for humping the couch—he gets up – throws a punch at me—and we get into it until everyone breaks it up. So yeah, the first time I got high was with those guys—smoking a water bong!"

**So that covers the drinking & smoking...**

"Oh, I got a good one about both—it was myself, the two Games Leads, and another friend, and we were all drunk—drunk as shit – and high – high as shit—and we go to Subway in Elgin. So I'm sitting there eating my Subway, and lo and behold, guess who shows up—my parents and brother."

*"So we were off in the corner and one of the Leads says: Why is that bitch looking at me?—Now, this lady happens to be my mother, so I told him to calm down. My step-dad comes over, and decides to start fucking with me. He brings me outside, and tells me that the entire house just got robbed—because I left the door open! After freak'n out for a bit, he tells me that it didn't, and that he was just bust'n my balls. It was a good lesson though, because we were all pretty much stoned and drunk—and figured it could have very well happened."*

**Did you ever get high in the park?**

*"I remember taking the shortcut through the train track sometimes—while people were actually riding the ride—and we would be smoke'n a joint back there!"*

**For many I heard from, those summers were the first time they experimented with sex, how bout you?**

*"Yes, I did pop my cherry there!"*

**Any other memorable encounters?**

*"There was one that said she was pregnant after we had sex. She was begging me to go fuck her, and I was like—maybe later—I was drinking, getting high, having a good time with friends, and my buddy punches me in the leg, and was like—go fuck her! So, I'm like fine – and I go fuck her in the back of my friend Buck's car—and they all end up watching! So she gets pissed, and tells me she's knocked up—and I'm freak'n out because I thought she was knocked up for like a week. During this time she proceded to date my buddy, and the two of us figured out by her*

*period cycle that she wasn't with child, and that the pregnancy was false – much to my relief."*

**During those summers, partying and women went hand in hand—anything else stand out?**

*"I pass out at this one party that started immediately after work, and woke up the next day with this chick grinding up on me! I'm late for work already, so I hurry up and get there, look down, and see this huge white stain on my work shorts. What is this toothpaste? What the fuck? I take a closer look, and I'm like – I'm pretty sure this isn't toothpaste. So basically some girl pretty much gave me a lap dance on my dark blue shorts, and I had to walk around with a "toothpaste stain"—the entire day. I didn't dare get a wet rag and water to just wipe it off – no way—it was a badge of honor! I don't even remember who it was!"*

# SQUATTING FOR DOLLARS

J ay Cramer recalled the time he threw a party at his parents' house where the lap dances were done by a profes-
sional: *"I think it the Fourth of July in 1990, and I was going to throw a pool party! It was one of the Games Leads 21st Birthday, and earlier that day everyone wanted to hire a stripper to come to the Polar Dome for him, but that was a no-go for obvious reasons. So one of the other Leads asks me if we can do it at my party after my folks went to bed. I agreed, and after they went asleep, we sneak the stripper in and we have everyone go into the garage. My parents never found out, but dur- ing the night my mom kept coming downstairs to ask us to be quiet, because my dad had to get up early for work. So I ask the Lead whose*

*idea this was to go talk to mom—to which his response was—Tell her there's a stripper here, it's a 21st birthday!—He then realized how that would go over and proceeded to go inside, drunk off his ass, and try to calm her down. It turns out that it worked, and she went back to bed. If she had come out into the garage, she would have seen at least five guys lying on their backs with rolled up dollar bills in their mouths, just waiting for a nasty-ass stripper to walk over to them, squat on their face and pick up her pay with her money grabber! Ahhhhh The Village—learned more there than I did in high school!"*

**T**his was my response to Jay after reading his recollection: *Believe it or not, I was actually one of the five guys on their backs with money in mouth! Man, I totally forgot about that party—reading it just now made the memories come flooding back. Wow, that was almost nineteen years ago, and I somehow had that sordid night stored somewhere in the recesses of my brain. The night is obviously a little foggy, but I distinctly remember that the stripper wanted twenty dollar bills to be rolled up, but some of us drunk fools, me included, rolled up singles instead! On a side note, I was pretty sure most of the money she made that night was from what some of us game operators happened to take "on the side" that day at the Village!*

# NIGHTTIME NINJAS

When the sun went down, Jay's pool parties weren't the only place stealthy after-hours activities took place. Many employees remembered some late night Racing Rapids rendezvous.

* "There were a couple of times we would jump the fence, and go start up the Go-Karts at Racing Rapids. It was pitch dark, and we didn't know where the fuck we were going, driving around and hitting shit – we're lucky we didn't kill anybody!"

* "There was many times where we would hop the fence at night and partake in a little late night relaxation in the Lazy River. Who wants to deal with customers when you can have the whole thing to yourself?"

* "We actually used to treat Racing Rapids like our own private skateboard park at night. Me and a few guys would skate down the tube slide & ollie into the splash pool!"

* "What could be better then not having to pay or having to deal with the crowds by sneaking into the water park at night? The best part was that suits were optional!"

* "Getting drunk & high and then traversing down the water slides at night made for some VERY memorable occasions!"

# THIS IS YOUR BRAIN, THIS IS YOUR BRAIN ON...

**A**n employee who worked at the Ice Cream Shop found interesting ways to kill time...among other things: *"The movie Cocktail came out one summer when I worked there, so we would all practice flipping the whipped cream cans like Tom Cruise in front of the customers. We actually put on a pretty good show! When the customers were not around, we would suck the gas out of the cans. Wouldn't you?"*

**I**n the seventies, a former Grounds worker recalled experiencing some surreal sights: *"After one of our shifts ended me and a buddy had the bright idea to take a couple tabs of acid for shits and giggles. We went off into the woods behind The English Rotor till nightfall, and then came back in to explore the park while it was empty all night. I can't begin to explain some of the disturbing sights we witnessed during those eight hours..."*

**O**ne guy asked if anyone got incredibly baked, and tried walking around Santa's Village at night: *"Too creepy—with those snowmen afoot!"*

# Smoke It If You Got It

## By Christopher Dearman

**W**hile on the subject of getting high, another "first" of mine that took place during the Santa's Village years, was when I tried marijuana for the first time. I'm not sure why it took so long to experiment with pot, as it had been offered to me many times the summer before, but I had always passed on the chance to take a puff due to my nervousness of what to expect. Knowing that eventually I would work up the nerve to finally try it, I finally broke down at a party my second season working.

We were at a party that was being thrown at the home of a kid who was new to the Games Department that season. He was a year younger, but had an older brother who was a Lead in the Rides Department, so he was quickly accepted into the group. The party was sort of a mash-up of various-aged employees and departments. I had no idea where their mother was, but at the time she had a house filled with underage kids drinking and doing God knows what.

The girls were drinking two-liters filled with Purple Passion. The guys were drinking the obligatory Miller Lite, and fun times were being had by all. I quickly caught a good buzz from my low tolerance at the time, so when a buddy mentioned that someone had brought some of the green herb, I figured I might as well pop that cherry.

A group of us went outside, and I don't know who had the bright idea to go stand on the sidewalk in front of the house, but there stood five or six of us in a circle passing a joint and smoking cigarettes. Even buzzed, I remember being extremely nervous at the thought of partaking. I quietly asked a friend standing next to me what I should do, and he said it's like smoking a cigarette but to just hold the smoke in your lungs for as long as possible. When it came my turn to toke, heeding the advice of my buddy, I made it a personal challenge to keep the smoke in longer then anyone else. I almost fainted from trying so hard! The joint kept being passed, and I remember thinking to myself that there wasn't much to it. What was I so scared of all these years? I wasn't freaking out or hallucinating. I had just become extremely relaxed and learned what it felt like to be stoned.

As luck would have it, right in the middle of taking a huge hit from the joint my third or fourth time, one of Elgin's finest slowly drove past the group. Paranoia having settled in, we all scattered, and I quickly ran back into the house. It was only then did I realize that I had yet to exhale the large amount of smoke that was still in my lungs. I didn't dare go back outside for fear of the cops, so I looked around, and then quietly exhaled the smoke from my lungs into the red cotton curtains of the front bay window.

After covertly disposing of the smoke, I went to the garage to get a beer, and then went back inside to see if I could get into the game of poker that was running in the kitchen. I was just about to sit down when suddenly the older brother burst into the front door of the house, yelling that his mom just pulled up in the driveway and everyone needed to run out the back. He stood in the foyer directing traffic, but after a moment sniffed the air around him. Only then realizing what had taken place, he yelled: *"Which one of you fuck'n assholes exhaled pot in my mother's house!"* Not daring to admit to any transgressions, I didn't say a word, and took this as a sign that the party was over. I quickly left from the door out back, and I'm pretty sure that was the last time those two ever had an employee party.

"I used to get high on the Sky Ride!"
- Former Grounds Employee

# LIONS & TIGERS & MONKS—OH MY

**L**isa Meadows Lyss, who worked at Santa's Village the summer of 1985, recalled the night she experienced one of the ever-changing urban legends of Sunset Road that was located near the park: *"When the season was under way, my friend and I were told that we needed to be initiated into the Games Department. So, we all met up after work and hung out until the time of our initiation. Like faithful sheep, we followed everyone to the top of Sunset. (also known as Monk Road) Folklore said there was a house on Monk Road that housed a murderous monk. Our initiation was to walk down Monk Road, walk up to the house and ring the doorbell. It was crazy scary. The road was dark, and you heard all sorts of animals moving in the brush. When we got near the Monk's house, a couple of the senior members jumped out and scared the living daylights out of us. We ran all the way back to our cars screaming!*

# The Nerve of This Guy

## By Christopher Dearman

Speaking of screaming, I have to preface this by saying that I am not proud of what I'm about to describe, but it is kind of funny in a *what was I thinking?* sort of way. It was Saturday afternoon, one where I knew my parents were not going to be home for many hours, so I decided to have a summer get-together with a dozen or so employees from The Village. I don't recall much of this particular afternoon, but what I do remember is something I still feel bad about to this day.

Sitting on the sectional couch in my basement and feeling no pain after a few beers, I remember looking around to see quite a few faces that I didn't recognize. Not that this was a problem as I always was up for meeting new people, but as it was my parents' home, I needed to keep an eye out to make sure everyone was kept in check.

Shooting the shit with my friend who we'll call "Dustin," I noticed this strange kid I never saw before sitting a few spots down from me with a glazed look to his eyes, not really talking much. I asked Dustin what this kid's story was—as the dude was seriously starting to weird me out by seemingly staring off into nothingness. Knowing that I would have no problem calling this kid out in my own home for being so odd, Dustin leaned in and whispered to me to take it easy on him. He informed me that it was a kid from his high school who worked at Santa's Village, and that one day last season he was working the Shooting Gallery and evidently got electrocuted by one of the machines that ran all the moving targets!

This was the first time I had ever heard of such a thing, I asked how something like this could possibly not be known to everyone. At the least, it would be in all the local newspapers, if not the lead story on the evening news. He said the reason why no one knew about it was that Santa's Village settled out of court for something like fifty thousand dollars to keep things quiet, as well as allowing him to keep a job working at the park as long as he wanted.

"50K!"—I replied, exasperated at the thought of so much money at that age. "Shit, I'd take a few volts to the arm for that much!" Dustin answered back with a surprised look—"Are you fuckin' kidding me? The guy has absolutely no feeling in his arm!"

Now, Dustin had been known to throw out a line of B.S. a time or two, and not believing that this sort of thing was even possible, my gut was cautioning me that he was probably trying to punk my ass. "You expect me to believe that this guy doesn't have ANY feeling in his left arm?" Extensive nerve damage or not, this was a bit hard for me to swallow. "The guy has to feel something!"—I pleaded, lighting up a cigarette with a Zippo lighter I had earned by saving up promotional Camel Bucks all summer. "You're telling me if I held this lighter under his arm, that he wouldn't know it was under there?" Dustin looked me in the eye with a straight face and says: "I'm telling you, man—he don't feel shit!"

Sounded like a bet to me. Calling bullshit, I told him to put his money where his mouth was. "Twenty bucks the kid yells like a little baby within ten seconds of me holding this lighter under his fore-arm." Dustin tells me it's not possible, and eagerly takes the bet.

With game on, I covertly went to go get another beer, then casually sat down beside the kid who looked like a patient from the movie One Flew Over the Cuckoo's Nest. I had my back to him at this point, and struck up a conversation with someone to the left of me—all the time preparing to make my move. Slowly, I started swiveling around a bit to get a better angle. I'll be honest, I did have second thoughts about doing this, but I figured if Dustin was telling the truth, the kid wouldn't feel anything. If he wasn't, I'd still make a half day's pay right from my own couch.

By this time Dustin had gathered a few other people off to the side to witness this vile experiment. I have to say that the curiosity was killing me, and at the time it seemed like valid research into the science of the human body. So, with my morals obviously taking a mini siesta, I sneakily snuck the lighter underneath his left forearm and flicked it ablaze.

Holding the flame of the lighter underneath his forearm literally about a centimeter from his skin, I mentally began to count to ten. I started to feel bad when black smoke started rising about five seconds into it, but there was no turning back now – I was only five seconds away from being twenty dollars richer!

Now, I can't tell you if it was from the kid just noticing the lit flame or from him actually feeling it burn his flesh, but just before the ten second mark the guy breaks out of his daze and jumps from the couch—*"What the FUCK are you doing!"* Dustin and the rest of the crew watching fall out laughing, and I was left there bug-eyed, not really having any plausible explanation for deliberately attempting to light the poor kid on fire.

Apologizing profusely at my childish behavior, I attempted to calm him down. I tried explaining my reasoning for treating him like Joan of Arc, but not unexpectedly, the guy wanted nothing to do with my feeble attempts to pacify him. I watched him storm out to the back porch where a bunch of girls were hanging out, and while I can't read lips, I'm pretty sure he started telling everyone what an asshole I was.

Feeling terrible, I went to Dustin to collect the bet, and then made my way back out to find the burn victim. Hoping to ease my guilty conscience while attempting to dodge the icy stares I'm getting from all the girls, I went up to the kid and handed over the twenty dollars I just won. I realized this didn't make up for my foolish actions, but in my mind at least I didn't profit from them either.

I'm not sure if the kid ever forgave me, but if he happens to ever read this, please understand that I'm truly sorry for my childish behavior. I'll even let you know that just now while writing this, I lit a lighter underneath my own forearm for you as payback. Granted, I pulled it away after five seconds – that shit hurt—but hopefully you'll consider that a little bit of retribution for the memorable story.

As a postscript to this, while interviewing people I used to work with all those years ago, I asked one of my old friends if he remembered anything from this incident. He said he didn't recall the bet as he may not have been there that day, but he definitely remembered the kid in question: "*We went to the same high school, and supposedly he was working the game, reached behind something, and started touching the wires. He sued the place because he was electrocuted, and then all the time in high school he would ask people to bang on his hands because he didn't have any feelings. So, we would pound the shit out of his hands, and he claimed he couldn't feel any of it. This continued all throughout high school where he would complain about not having any feelings in his hands, and I'm like—Well, it's because you're a dumb-ass, I mean, why you reaching behind all this electrical equipment?*"

# ✪ ACCIDENTS & MISHAPS ✪

In the past twenty years I have heard many stories from people about the numerous accidents and deaths that supposedly happened at Santa's Village. People jumping off the Sky Ride to commit suicide; heads getting decapitated while standing up on the Typhoon roller coaster, or strangulation of scarf-wearers whose scarf got caught in a ride's gears are just a few of the many casualties people are convinced happened over the years the park was open.

I have also heard detailed descriptions of multiple child kidnapping attempts, AIDs-infected drug syringes stuck into ride seats, and poisonous snake dens found at the bottom of the plastic ball pit. While many people are convinced that there were secret payoffs to victims to keep things out of newspapers and the evening news, I have found that most of these rumors would have to fall into the category of an urban legend.

While interviewing Phil Wenz for the book, I was very anxious to see if he could shed some light on some of these things, as I was sure it would make for some juicy stories. Unfortunately, at least for the entertainment value that such stories would bring, he shot down most as either happening at other amusement parks or made up all together.

He was able to provide information on some of the few accidents that really did happen. Surprisingly, given the park's long-running history, I would have guessed that there would have been substantially more, but it seems not to be the case. Besides the typical cuts, bruises, sprains and other minor injuries that happen at most amusement parks over time, major incidents were few and far between.

The most well-known of these accidents came back in 1993, when a women was killed in a freak accident that involved the Candy Cane Sleigh ride. While the details of what exactly caused the horses pulling the sleigh to go out of control, and whether there was anything the seventeen-year-old operator could have done to prevent it are up for debate, the unfortunate outcome was that a fatal head injury did occur.

**Phil Wenz remembered that day vividly:** *"That was a weird day. I'm not sure what caused the horses to bolt that day, but my understanding of that situation is that I was working in Santa's House, and it happened right after the park opened. We saw all the Management come out of the main office and charge to the back of the park, so we knew something had happened. Shortly thereafter, someone came in and told us that there had been an accident in the park; the sleigh tipped over, and they weren't sure what caused it."*

*"One of the managers came in the house to take a break, and told us that there was a helicopter hovering over the park across the street, and a bunch of news crews had arrived. From my understanding of what happened was that the horse-drawn sleigh was coming around the corner, went into the tunnel, and I guess once in the tunnel the horses really increased speed—I mean really took off. By the time it went around the back stretch the driver could not get them under control, and the thing tipped on the last curve, over the embankment where the barn is. On the last curve that thing just let loose and just rolled off. The horses went down, and everyone just tumbled out. It ended up that the lady hit her head and died."*

*"So the ambulances came in the back way. Police taped everything off; closed the ride for the investigation, and everything just went back to normal. It was just a weird day. A lot of people didn't even know about it. It happened first thing in the morning. They set up benches to close off that whole area of the park until the investigators were done. They were there for like an hour and a half, but eventually opened everything back up. They may have run the ride again, but I know by 1994 it was gone."*

**When I asked Phil about a well-known drowning that occurred in the Swan Pond after hours, he had this recollection:** *"What happened there, from what I can gather, is that some kids were trespassing, climbed over the fence to go swimming, and one of the kids drowned. Officials ended up having to dredge the pond to find the body. It was one of those things where I don't think there was any charges brought. He was seventeen years old, trespassing, and shouldn't have been there."*

**When asked if he knew of any other deaths besides the sleigh, Phil recalled hearing about the time a young girl unfortunately**

**decided to not stay seated in a moving ride**: *"It was 1981 and apparently, from what I have read, there was a tragic accident on the Silver Streak ride involving a young girl. I guess she wanted to get into the compartment behind her and she stood up. The way the ride worked is that all the gears were in the middle of the ride and when she stood up to get in the back compartment, the ride sucked her right into it, and that was it. I don't think anything litigious happened at the time. This was 1981 and people weren't suing then."*

**What about the guy who jumped off the Sky Ride and committed suicide?** *"I know people would jump off at the one end where it was like twenty feet high, just to save them a trip to Coney Island because you couldn't get off there, but as for someone jumping off to commit suicide—not to my knowledge. That was an urban legend. I think that might have happened at one of the Six Flags parks. A lot of times when things happened at other parks they inevitably were told that they happened at Santa's Village."*

**M**ark Bloomer witnessed many accidents and near accidents during his five seasons working at The Village when he was a Rides manager: *"I remember getting a radio call about the Fire Truck breaking down. As I headed over, the operators were walking the guests back to the entrance. They said the truck was over-heating. I walked down toward it and noticed the white smoke was turning dark. Right away I knew we had a problem. The truck was*

*on fire! I made my calls on the radio, and ran down to the bumper
cars to grab an extinguisher. When I got back the thing was burning. I
shoved the extinguisher hose in the grille and pulled the trigger—didn't
do a damn thing. The truck kept burning till the real fire truck came
and put it out."*

**Luckily no one was hurt. Did you witness any injuries during
your time there?**

*"Watched the Typhoon train break apart and crash into each other!
People got some whiplash. When it rained people would run on the
Tilt-O-Whirl platform and it was like ice -watched people fly on their
ass. I sustained some smoke inhalation when the Fire Truck went up
in flames. Yes...the Fire Truck. Burnt my hands when I pulled off the
Yo-Yo panels and it went up in flames."*

**Anyone else ever get hurt?**

*"It was a real busy day at The Village so all employees were asked to
park by the pond by Dunkin Donuts. Well, we end up closing early cuz
of bad weather. Me and a buddy walk down to the lot to leave. We walk
up to the gate to find it locked with a chain and padlock. My buddy goes
to grab the chain right as lighting strikes the tree next to us. I watched
sparks fly off the chain and lock as my buddy held it! Scared the shit
out of me. I ran and didn't look back. To this day I have a serious fear
of lighting because of that."*

**How about any close calls?**

*"I remember me and another Rides manager were up in the Coney
Island part of the park when over my shoulder, I noticed the lifts on the*

*Skyliner were swinging violently. As I watched, one of the lifts broke away from the cable! It hit the ground and broke to pieces—I shit a brick! The next lift had a man with his young boy on it. I don't think I've ever ran so fast. I ran the whole length of the Skyliner, leaping fences, over the railroad, dodged the antique cars, and had the operators shut down the ride. Thank God, we didn't load another chair lift!"*

*"I also remember walking past the main gate and turning to see a snowball from the Snowball ride rolling around with people in it. The thing broke off and started doing what any ball would do—roll!"*

O ther employees have their own recollections of accidents, mishaps and urban legends they either claim to have witnessed or heard about. Some of them verifiable, some obviously not:

* "I was not nearly old enough to be involved in either hijinx nor debauchery at Santa's Village, but I did knock out a front tooth in a nasty fall there!"

* "I did see a guy have his hand skated over - that was a mess on the ice!"

* "I heard about this one guy that got all drunk and fell off the Sky Ride. He landed right on top of that elephant statue! The elephant now resides at that bar in East Dundee called Bandito Barneys and I hear if you look real closely - you can still see remnants of the dude's blood on it!"

✳ "There was this one summer we worked where all these animals on the farm started dying off. I think it was some sort of plague or something.

✳ "I will never forget hearing the news of my friend Brenden involved in the horrible accident while working on the Fire Truck ride. The truck started off, and he wasn't on the back yet. So he had run to jump on and slipped, I believe on the wet cement, and ended up under the truck—which ran him over. I was in shock when I heard, and was really shaken up the rest of the day. He was hurt pretty bad, and never returned to work. He survived, and we continued being friends for some time."

✳ "I remember going over to the Evergreen Theater during my breaks before the park opened to ogle at some of the hot singer chicks in those skimpy costumes. My hormones were raging at the time, and I always wanted to catch some of those rumored orgies. Never got to witness anything scandalous though—except maybe catching a glimpse of a bra or something."

✳ "I heard that there were cops on FOP day that would wear their gun, going down the water slides! Also that some lady lost a huge diamond ring in the lazy river. It never showed up though—was it in the filters?"

* "I burned my feet badly when I dropped
boiling water on them while trying to get
the hot dog steamers ready one morning.
I still have a scar on my big toe from the
burn!"

* "Injuries? I sprained my leg while trying
to jump from one of those old time cars
onto another while they were moving."

* "Man, I heard that one of the Santa's would
have to get sauced all the time in order
to deal with all those brats! That he had
a stash of moonshine or some shit that he
kept behind his chair, and would just take
swigs from it throughout the day."

* Jay Crammer, when asked if he heard of
any urban legends replied: "Bob Flink-
anything he ever said!"

# CHAPTER EIGHT

# ALL GOOD THINGS COME TO AN END

# POSTER PITCH SHAKEDOWN

## BY CHRISTOPHER DEARMAN

**B**esides being profitable to me in more ways than one, Poster Pitch also became the game that would bring an end to my Santa's Village career—but not in the way that you might expect. This is the story about my first time getting fired.

It was another beautiful day at the park during my second summer working at Santa's Village. I was now what you would consider a veteran, and even though I had been given a heads-up numerous times by the older Leads that I was being "watched" for suspicion of stealing, my confidence in my skills convinced me that I would never be caught.

I couldn't tell you what I was hoping to purchase on this particular day, but at the morning meeting I stuck to the standard procedure of trying to get one of the more profitable five-finger games. I ended up getting Poster Pitch, which everyone knew was one of the easier games to steal from. When I got to the game I immediately started in with the carnie act which managers love, and verbally assaulted every person who walked by trying to get them to pony up a dollar for a poster. *"You can't lose—everyone is a winner—no need for luck, it only costs a buck!"*

So I did my thing, and quickly had about sixty dollars in my pocket. During this time, a girl who used to go to my high school Freshman year happened to walk by as a paying customer. She was cute, but her blonde friend who was with her was drop-dead gorgeous, so of course I turned on the charm. There was a large crowd of people around me at the time, and in-between getting them to laugh at stupid jokes, I did some major flirting with the hottie. I was getting a good response and digging the smiles she was giving me. Since the game was doing gangbuster business, I told the two to go enjoy some rides and come back later when things calmed down. I *may* have suggested that I would give them whatever poster they wished when they came back.

So about an hour or so later they come back around, and the hottie flashed me that pretty smile again.

*"Go ahead and just throw a dart at whatever poster you two want."*—I said in my best Rico Suavé voice.

*"And we don't have to pay?"*—the blonde giggled.

*"No, don't worry about it."*—I said, looking around hoping she would hurry up already.

*"Well in that case, do you think I could get all the New Kids on the Block ones?"*—She batted her eyelashes in a way that I couldn't say no.

*"I want all of them too!"*—my former classmate chimed in.

Damn, a total of ten posters! These chicks got some nerve. I was only thinking one each, but it wasn't like I could say no now. I had each of them throw a dart at one of the five, and then went to the side room where all the posters were stored. Donny, Danny, Jordan, Joey and Jonathan—damn these chicks were greedy! I decided it would be best to just roll all five into one, so that it didn't look suspicious if anyone was watching when I handed them over. After spending considerable time putting everything together, I went back to the girls, and watched how the thrill of having a complete set of New Kids for their wall got them all sorts of excited.

The girls were happy as hell, and during their jubilation I told them to stop by before they leave so we could make plans to hang later. They said they definitely would, and started walking away. The hot girl turned back to flash me that smile one last time, and I was left standing there on Cloud Nine.

Turned out my happiness lasted for mere seconds as no sooner had they rounded the corner, a bunch of white shirts bum rushed me and came up to the game—security was with them. One of the Leads named Bob, who I had partied with many times before, was acting all professional and adult-like when he instructed me to hand over my money belt. I turned to my manager John and asked him what the hell was going on. He told me that I was to go with him to the front office.

"What for? I didn't steal anything!"—I said, lying to his face with a pocketful of twenties.

"You did steal. You stole the two posters that you just gave to those girls!"

"Are you fuck'n kidding me? I paid for those myself!"—a plan to get out of the predicament immediately formed in my head.

"What do you mean you paid for them? I was watching you—they didn't put anything in the lockbox."

"Check the belt! There is more than a hundred dollars in it. I just wanted to impress the girls so I let it seem like I was giving them the posters for free, but in reality, paid for them myself!"

Now there indeed was more then a hundred dollars in the belt. There actually was an extra five, but that money definitely was not mine—at least not yet anyway. Part of the technique I used to steal was to make change for customers, and instead of them putting the singles in the lockbox on the counter, I would just offer to do it for them. I could then slip a couple bucks at a time into the counter in case anyone was watching, but at the same time sneak out a couple on the sly. All it took was to keep a running tally of how much money I was up, and when the opportune time came when I knew no one was watching, just transfer it to my pocket.

After I spun my tale of how all of this was just a dumb misunderstanding, they all looked at each other like—what do we do now? What can we fire him for? Thinking I had gotten myself out of this jam, I wasn't too worried when John radioed one of the owners to relay my story. I was standing around thinking I had dodged a bullet, but then heard the crackle of the walkie-talkie say—*"Cuff him."*, and I was stunned to see the security guard start pulling out his handcuffs.

*"Is this really necessary, man?"*—I said to him, shocked that I was about to be treated like a common criminal. I had joked around with this particular security guard more than a few times, so I thought he would cut me a break. He apologized to me but said he had to follow orders, and tightly handcuffed me behind my back. It was only then that it hit me—this was going to be embarrassing.

So John and Bob went off to go do whatever they needed to do—I imagine celebrate—and the security guard started walking me to Games Alley. I stopped and asked for him to at least walk me around in the other longer direction so I wouldn't have to see my peers—and thankfully he did. I still remember the looks of bewilderment the customers walking around the park were giving me—customers who just a little while earlier had been laughing at my jokes and having a good time at my game. Now people were looking at me like I killed someone. I kept my head down, and quickly walked to front entrance with my security escort, hoping not to run into anyone I knew. With my luck, we walked right into the two girls that got me into this mess. They asked what happened, and I replied testily that I was getting fired for giving away posters—hoping to make the greedy bitches at least have a little guilt for wanting so damn many.

When I got to the front office I was brought in before one of the owners, and I again explained my bullshit story about how I wanted to impress the girls and had indeed paid for the posters. He informed me that they normally would bring in the authorities for what they consider stealing from the company, but that since I supposedly paid for them (and they knew that nothing would probably stick), that I would just be fired. My first real job, and I got fired. The kicker was that I didn't get canned for the few grand that I stole from them over the two summers, but for giving away posters that cost a few pennies—all in hopes to impress a girl. Go figure.

As a postscript to the story, later that evening there was a Santa's Village after-hours party where I ran into Bob and a couple of the other Leads. Immediately I started bitching them out for being in on this. *"How could you do this to me?"* Bob, with his obligatory big chaw in his lip, informed me that he had no choice in the matter. That I was being watched by Management for weeks, but they couldn't catch me in the act of stealing even though they knew I had to be. *"I have told you this plenty of times, Dearman, and I have even turned a blind eye more then once."*

Knowing that this was true I couldn't be too mad at him. He went on tell me that the whole day had been a sting to try and catch me—like they were the secret service, trying to avert an assassination attempt or some shit. They had Bob in the Polar Dome rafters—let me say that again—they had Bob in the *rafters*—staked out all day, sweating up in the ceiling above me, watching and informing my movements to Management by walkie-talkie. I guess one of the owners was watching me all day in the restaurant across from the Poster Pitch, looking through the glass windows where you couldn't see in but could easily see out. They even had the Games manager John watching me with *binoculars* from the forest area—I was under watch from all possible angles!

Bob said his hands were tied, he had to be a part of it, and reminded me that he had given me a heads-up earlier that week— one I so stubbornly disregarded. Being so young at the time I really didn't give much thought to being fired, and immediately went and got a slightly higher paying job working at Spring Hill Theater so that my parents couldn't question me too hard about why I wasn't working at Santa's Village anymore. Only now by reading this are they going to find out the real truth!

At the time I did get a good laugh out of all that went on to try to catch me, and especially loved that even through all their efforts to do so—I never did get caught for stealing. Probably the reason why Karma has paid me back more than once in my lifetime—to make me pay for my younger years' transgressions. By confessing to all my "sins" and telling my embarrassing stories from these two summers for all to read, hopefully Karma will take this into consideration before throwing any more drama my way...

# THE LAST DAY

## By Phillip L. Wenz

he last day that Santa's Village in Dundee, Illinois would be open to the public was on September 18, 2005. The Polar Dome shut its doors in May of 2006. Forty-six years had passed since my first predecessor "Santa" Jim Combs opened the gates to the Village in 1959. And fifty years had passed since the first "Santa's Village Santa" Carl Hansen opened the first of Glenn Holland's three Santa's Villages. Hansen opened up the Sky Forest, CA location in 1955 and he opened the second park in 1957 at Scotts Valley, CA. The Sky Forest Park was opened for forty-three years and closed in 1998, while the Scotts Valley's Park closed in 1978 after a twenty-one year run. Dundee outlasted them all with forty-six years.

I arrived at Santa's Village early that day in September of 2005. I wanted to take in the whole experience of that day. Rumors had been flying that the park was going to be sold and this was just another closing day. None of the people who worked at the park on that last day thought this was going to happen. And of course it did not.

This last day was a passing. A passing of a dream, the passing of magic and most importantly the passing of the people who worked at Santa's Village over the years. I could not help but think of these people as I began my day as Santa. I knew this might be the last time that I was in Santa's House, visiting guests and entertaining the young at heart.

It was a weird day from the start. A pretty good-sized crowd was there that day, all with cameras. In reality, more pictures were probably taken in the park that day than in any day in the last 40 years. People just soaked it all in.

By 1:00 pm you could see some of the Management of the park getting a little emotional because of the day. Visitors came and went in a steady pace all day in Santa's House. I kept my composure until Debbi, the long-time manager of the barn and petting zoo, came into Santa's House. Debbi, like a few others, had been associated with the park for decades. Her smiling face and tear-soaked eyes got to me.

Her visit made me realize what Santa's Village meant to a lot of people...family. Whether you worked out at the park in 1959, 1966, 1972, or whatever year, you were part of this extended family. During the last hours that Santa's House was open that day, mostly employees came in. It was all I could do to keep in character. When it came time to close up the house that day, I made sure I knew who the last visitors were and I had the last picture taken in the house.

Going to my dressing room when my day was finished, it was hard not to think of all the people who I had the good fortune of working with at the park. I thought of one of the owners who passed away a few years earlier and thought of Don the general manager of the park for so many years. Others crossed my mind such as Frank, John and Joslyn, Jill, Grant, Lori, Lauren, JoEllen, Luda, Pete, Cathy, and Toby. The Maintenance guys over the years, Ralph, Red, Bob, Kenny, Nels, Gene, Ron and Russ. The food service managers Willie and Marion Hankey. All these people and more were part of my time at the park.

I thought about all the people who worked there before me like "Santa" Don Goers and general manager Ray VanRoyen and Jack Morningstar. I thought about the original Santa's Village

Corporation folks, Glenn Holland and J.P. Henck. All were part of this day.

When I had finally changed out of my costume, I went and sat in the park with a lot of the Management who were winding this day down. The director of operations, Crystal, had been a part of this park for thirty years; the Maintenance Department of Gary, Mark and Matt; the current owner and his son and daughter-in -law and the security guards, Dean and Al were all around the Snowball ride. The park's wonderful magic act duo of Tim and Robin were there. Sue L. was there, smiling like she always did. Sue H. and Jeff D. were tucked away in guest services, preparing for the closing of the day.

When it came time for the closing announcement, we all just kind of looked at each other. When it was announced, I remember everyone dispersing, as the park had to be locked down. I sat on a bench with Tom, the Grounds manager, and watched as the people exited. Across from us sat the owner. I don't think a word was said.

As the last people exited, I thought about how over the years Santa's Village provided magic and entertainment for over twenty million guests. The owners, managers, contractors and thousands of local teenagers created that magic. All of them contributed to the forty-six years of Santa's Village.

When the park was secure, the managers met in the Polar Dome's Alpine Room. Everybody knew in their hearts that it was over. With the clinking of glasses, Santa's Village in Dundee passed into our collective memory.

# SANTA'S VILLAGE FACTS

## By Phillip L. Wenz

ark creator Glenn Holland insisted that theme presentation was important. Numerous static displays were in the park. Buildings and grounds were decorated with elaborate details. Even money never exchanged hands as a small passport ticket was used to keep track of the guest's expenses. The passport would be checked out at the end of the visit in the exit shop. Children's belief in the myth was paramount.

Holland also created his own line of branded products. Storybooks, puzzles, and coloring books could be bought at the park as well as in stores throughout the region. The Santa's Village candies were sold via mail order.

The mushrooms and toadstools? Holland wanted his visitors' experience to be so complete that these brightly colored concrete creations dotted the landscape. Why? In Norwegian legend, the Vindicans (little people) who were craftsmen lived in the toadstools and mushrooms. Pixies and Elves along with Gnomes are a direct relative to the Vindican. Holland gave all of Santa's helpers a place to live in the "Village."

# Santa's Village Owners

(1959) Santa's Village Corp. of California / Glenn Holland and General Contractor J. P. Henck

(1965) Everding Management / Durell Everding

(1972) Medina Investors / Barney Clark

(1978) North Pole Corporation / Hugh D. Wilson and Philip Oestreich

# Santa's Village General Managers

| | |
|---|---|
| Charles L. Poe | (1959-1962) |
| Raymond J. Van Royen | (1962-1963) |
| Jack R. Morningstar | (1963-1972) |
| Donald L. Holliman | (1972-2003) |
| Hugh D. Wilson | (2004-2005) |

# Santa's Village 1959

**What Santa's Village looked like on opening day May 30, 1959.**

**Entrance House/Exit Shop** — A multipurpose building that also housed the general offices of Santa's Village Corporation. (Offices are on the second floors of both ends of the building.) The actual entrance into the park was in the south end of the building where Guest Services is today. The Exit Shop composes the middle and north end of the lower level.

**North Pole** – A six-foot pillar of ice that stood near the center of the park. The North Pole area was referred to as "North Pole Plaza" and was surrounded by cement snow on the east and west sides. The North Pole has been in three different locations in the park's history.

**Santa's House** – Children could visit Santa and sign his Good Book.

**Doll House** – A shop that contained unique dolls and accessories from all over the world.

**Pixie Pantry** – The park's largest eating facility that served sit-down meals cafeteria style in the main section and hamburgers, hotdogs, and typical fast food through a walk-up window.

**Chapel of the Little Shepard** – A small, all-faith chapel that reflected on children's bible stories through small exhibits.

**Wee Puppet Theatre** – Daily hand and marionette puppet shows in an indoor theatre.

**Reindeer Barn** – Santa's reindeer actually lived in the barn. There were eight stalls and at the north end of the barn, "Inky" the reindeer, along with his friends "Peck" the chicken and "Hunt" the duck printed the park's official newspaper, *The Pixie Press*.

**Igloo** – A small concrete "igloo" that originally served small ice cream novelties.

**Santa's Gift Shop** – One of the largest buildings in the park, the shop was divided into three sections, toys for children, gifts for moms and dads, and a Christmas shop.

**Storybook House** – A small shop that handled children's books and souvenirs.

**Jack-in-the-Box** – A snow cone stand that looked like its name.

**Easter Bunny Hut** – A large walk-through, egg-shaped house.

**Mrs. Claus' Candy Kitchen** – A large building that was a candy shop that sold hand-dipped chocolates and hard candies. Mrs. Claus was on hand each day to supervise.

**Millwheel Workshop (Santa's Workshop)** – An artisan's shop that also sold manufactured toys.

**Gingerbread House** – An actual working bakery that featured gingerbread cookies and baked goods. Large windows allowed guests to watch as "Pixies" made the sweet treats. The Gingerbread House was also home to the "Good Witch" and the "Lollipop Lady." Right behind the outside fireplace, children could accompany the "Lollipop Lady" and pick a sucker from the lollipop tree.

**Christmas Around the World Post Office** – A large building that housed many an exhibit and services such as an actual post office, letter writing to Santa, exhibit windows of the celebrations of Christmas around the world, a souvenir counter, guest services, and restrooms. Offices were located on the second floor.

**The Toy Soldier** – A giant toy drum with a tall toy soldier on top that was actually a "duck pond game" with little toy boots instead of rubber ducks.

**Wishing Well** – A small outdoor seating area where folks could relax and children could drop pennies into a well for a secret wish.

**Tree House Slide** — A tree house that featured a staircase up to a small hut where children find a slide to come down. The slide ends in a sand box.

**Silver Slipper Pond** — A pond that featured a small castle to walk through and a bridge to cross.

**Woodanimals** – Large wooden log sculptures that children could sit and climb on.

**Cinderella's Pumpkin Coach** – A life-sized coach that guests could ride in that was pulled by miniature white ponies. The turn-a-round area contained a static display of Prince Charming's Castle.

**Burro Ride** – Children could ride on a live burro through the forest.

**Magic Train** – A small locomotive train traveled through the magic forest's "Land of Enchantment" that had numerous static displays.

**Candy Cane Sleigh Ride** – Guests could ride in a sleigh

pulled by Santa's Reindeer that took them on a journey through icecaps and the "Elves' Village" in search of the "Snow Queen."

**Christmas Tree Ride** – A giant whirling tree where guests could ride in a Christmas ornament that would go up and down with the pull of a lever.

**Gasoline Powered Tractors** – Actual small tractors that children could drive around a small farm set-up.


# Live Characters

Santa Claus

Mrs. Claus

The Good Witch

The Lollipop Lady

Jack Pumpkin Head

Mr. Bunny (Easter Bunny)

Cinderella (Pumpkin Princess)

General employees were dressed as "Pixies and/or Elves"

Live Animals

Santa's team of reindeer (Candy Cane Sleigh Ride)

Inky the reindeer, Hunt the duck and Peck the chicken (*The Pixie Press*)

Two teams of four white ponies (Pumpkin Coach)

Numerous burros, goats, and petting zoo animals

# Santa's Village 2005

**Santa's Village as it was on September 18, 2005:**

Santa's Village Theme Park, located in the beautiful Fox River Valley, is the place to find traditional amusement park family fun at a price the modern family can afford. Close to home, with plenty of free parking, over 40 rides, shows and attractions, and spacious picnic areas, all in a beautiful relaxed country setting, Santa's Village is the perfect place for quality family fun and memories.

Santa's Village has been a favorite family tradition for 46 years. With thrill and kiddie rides, live shows, and attractions, there's something for everyone. The park is divided into three areas that have fun, excitement, and entertainment for all ages!

# Santa's World

There is kids stuff galore in Santa's World, home of the original Snowball Ride and the Frozen North Pole! There are games of skill in the Midway and lots of pint-sized fun to enjoy. Take to the road on the Convoy, or blaze a high-speed trail of fun on Dracor, the Dragon Coaster!

# And don't forget to visit Santa in his North Pole Home!

For 46 years Santa's House inside Santa's Village Theme Park has been home to jolly old St. Nick! This storybook cottage has been host to hundreds of thousands of children who spend that magical moment with Santa Claus. Filled with antiques, set near the center of the park, the house is a nostalgic example of old-time Christmas spirit and hospitality.

When venturing up to Santa's House, one can see and touch the frozen North Pole right outside the front door. The "Pole" stays icy even on the hottest summer days. At the front door a giant key unlocks the secrets of the home to visitors. Inside you can see Santa's sleigh loaded with Christmas goodies, a beautiful tree that stays up all year long and the huge cobblestone fireplace that warms the home on those "cold winter nights." Children can sit at Santa's desk and sign his Good Book. Twinkle lights, decorations, and wrapped packages adorn the rafters.

Imagine the look on a child's face when he or she comes into this house of real make-believe! Santa talks and visits with everyone just as he has since the "Village" opened in 1959. Santa's House is the home of all that makes childhood fantasy a magical memory for children of all ages.

## Petting Zoo at Old McDonald's Farm

Walk, talk, and mingle with the animals down at the Petting Zoo. A wide variety of animals are featured throughout the barn and in the barnyard. Laugh while children feed the silly pygmy goats and all the animals. From rabbits to llamas, there's a friendly face waiting for you.

## Coney Island

Coney Island offers a world of excitement in the air and on the ground. Towering 63 feet high, the TYPHOON Roller Coaster will turn you upside down and blow you away! Become a mate on the Galleon Pirate Ship. This 18th Century replica will take you on a high seas adventure as you pendulum over 40 feet in the air. Or tingle with excitement on other thrill rides like the Great Wheel, Yo-Yo, Himalaya, Skyliner, or Dodge 'Em Bumper Cars!

## Santa's Snowstorm Game Show

A thrilling game show where randomly selected audience members participate in wild and crazy games. The final winner enters the snowstorm chamber and grabs "Santa Bucks" as they swirl about. Catch the fun, excitement, and prizes! Please arrive at least 5-10 minutes prior to show time to be eligible as a contestant. You could be the big winner! This show takes place in the Evergreen Theater.

# Boardwalk Magic Review

Take a break and enjoy spellbinding illusion and comedic wit during this very entertaining 20 minute show by master magicians Tim and Robin Balster. This performance is at the outdoor theater at the end of the Midway.

# ✪ ACKNOWLEDGMENTS ✪

First of all, I would like to thank Phil Wenz. I owe you a huge debt of gratitude for providing me with a wealth of information on the park, the people who worked there, and with the whole process of making my vision a reality. Thank you for understanding that I wrote this book with good intentions, although many people thought otherwise. I am forever grateful.

Next I would like to thank James Hislope for turning my vision into an amazing looking cover. I can't tell you how many times looking at your work inspired me to continue working on this project to completion. I can't thank you enough for once again helping me bring the thoughts in my mind to a reality.

I would also like to thank Joey Campos for coloring James' art, turning his line drawings into the vibrant, colorful work of art it is today. You also did a great job on the back cover!

A very special thanks to Casey Hooper for her extreme patience and hard work in taking my words, ideas and ridiculous whims - and making them look highly professional with her amazing interior book design. I know she had to be cussing me out often...

My gratitude goes out to all those who took the time to submit their stories, memories, quotes and thoughts of their time working at Santa's Village. It was great having others share stories that helped spread out all my embarrassing ones! (even to those who were too scared to use their full names) I hope you enjoy seeing your words in print for prosperity—and feel free to buy many, many copies of the book to help spread the word—it makes a great Christmas gift! Among them are:

Michael Reeves, Dave Dekker, Ryan O., George Strissel, Debbie, Karen DeBias, Christopher French, Tami, Chris Morgan, John McMillin, Jay Cramer, Joshua Clark, Barbara Ulrich, Matthew Sparks, Ti'ara Wendt-Rozell, Tricia Kerrigan, Sarah Novak, Sheli R., Beth V., Brian Ruden, Vicky, Shannon Jacobs, Tania Binning, Andy Esch, Ann Fox, Matt Ferguson, Jennifer Miller-Riggs, Kelly Aniballi, Lisa Meadows Lyss, Meghan Earsley Williams, Janice Larson, J.J., Mark A. Bloomer, and T.J. 'The Governor' Lewis.

I also would like to thank the *many* who took part, but choose to keep themselves anonymous. After reading some of your stories— I completely understand!

There would have never even been a book if it wasn't for seeing the faces of some of my former fellow employees while surfing Facebook last year. Seeing them made a ton of memories come flooding back, inspiring me to put this book together. Here is a small list of those people, as well others I worked with or who played a part in some of the memories I shared throughout the book:

Justin, Brad, Becky, Brandi, Rhea, Lisa, Sara, Theresa, Dirk, Shane, Strawberry, Leslie, Jason, Bob, John, Pat, Tim, Tammy, Colleen, Jon, Jenny, Jason M., Christy, Chad, Dana, Adam, Starla, Liz, Jeff, Dan, Fred, Chris, Michelle, and being it's been nearly two decades since my days working at Santa's Village, I know I forgot the names of dozens more—so please forgive me.

Also, thanks to all the former owners and managers of Santa's Village throughout the years for providing the opportunity to work at such a unique place and allowing us to have such a fun time doing it.

I'd also like to thank some of the people that had a hand in either the creation and promotion of the book, or for providing insight and inspiration:

Anthony Filomena, DeAnn Johnson-Wenz, Denise Dorman, Sharon F. Kissane, Ph.D., Amber Gallagher, Greg Schwipps, Emily McFarlan, Katie Anderson & Kimmie Brakeall, Melissa Graham, Melissa Jornd, Jennifer Bradley, Aaron Krager, Stephanie Beavers, Sally La Luzerne-Oi, Lin Pflederer, Michele Carla, Jennifer Campbell, Timothy Ferriss, Joe Eszterhas, Chad Kultgen, Koren Zailckas, Kevin Smith, Perez Hilton, Chelsea Handler, Jenny McCarthy, Tucker Max, Stephanie Tomzak, Kimberly Ann Smith Photography, and a double thanks to Noreen Cottrell.

While on the subject of thanking people, I could have never written this book without the personal support of my friends, extended family, and others who have crossed paths with me one way or another on this journey called life. I started to compile a list of you all, but my back is killing me...so I just gave up. You know who you are—so thanks for everything!

Patty, thanks for all the years you spent putting up with me while trying to get my many creative endeavors out there—I truly appreciate it.

To my boys BillyD and Furly—thanks for putting up with the many days and nights of neglect while I was writing this thing. I owe you each a can of tuna.

Special thanks to my sister Ashlee—thanks for keeping me laughing!

And to wrap this up, my biggest thanks of all goes to my mom and dad. I know I have put you two through much more stress and heartache over the years than either of you deserved for deciding to bring me into this world...and I'm sure some of the stories in this book are going to add to that list, but thank you so much for your love and support. I love you both.

*Chris's first day of work - May 1990*

*From the author of SANTA'S VILLAGE GONE WILD!*

# Carbondale GONE WILD!

## Tales of college fun, hijinx & debauchery
## as told by the people who survived it
### by Christopher Dearman

**CARBONDALE GONE WILD!–** is a revealing look at some of the fun, hilarious & outrageous stories that took place over the many decades college students have been attending what formerly was known as one of the nations leading "party" schools.

We can now lift the curtain to let people know what REALLY went down while students were away from home...

While it's party image may be a thing of the past, stories of the infamous Halloween riots, the taking of The Strip, as well as numerous other rowdy tales of revelry for which it earned a place on Playboy magazine's top party list more then once will be revealed.

Christopher Dearman shares numerous stories of his years spent working on getting a degree, and all the hijinx & debauchery that went along with it. He also collects quotes & memories submitted by many other alumni that will paint an uncensored look at some of the coming of age stories that took place in Southern Illinois over the years.

### Visit:
## WWW.CARBONDALEGONEWILD.COM
### today for more info!